WHAT'S YOUR
INVESTING
IQ?

By
Carrie L. Coghill, CFP
With
Evan Pattak

THE CAREER PRESS, INC.
Franklin Lakes, NJ

0319726

WHAT'S YOUR INVESTING IQ?
EDITED BY KATE PRESTON
TYPESET BY EILEEN DOW MUNSON
Cover design by Cheryl Cohan Finbow
Printed in the U.S.A. by Book-mart Press

To order this title, please call toll-free 1-800-CAREER-1 (NJ and Canada: 201-848-0310) to order using VISA or MasterCard, or for further information on books from Career Press.

The authors and publisher specifically disclaim any responsibility for liability, loss or risk, personal or otherwise, that is incurred as a consequence, directly or indirectly, of the use and application of any of the contents of this book.

The Career Press, Inc., 3 Tice Road, PO Box 687,
Franklin Lakes, NJ 07417
www.careerpress.com

Library of Congress Cataloging-in-Publication Data

Coghill, Carrie L., 1965-
  What's your investing IQ? / by Carrie L. Coghill with Evan Pattak.
    p. cm.
  Includes bibliographical references and index.
  ISBN 1-56414-632-4 (paper)
    1. Investments. 2. Portfolio management. 3. Investment analysis.
  I. Pattak, Evan M. II. Title.

HG4521 .C5292 2003
  332.6—dc21

2002034895

Acknowledgments

The subjects of economics and investing are dynamic and complex, though we in the profession sometimes lose sight of just how dynamic and complex they are. I began to appreciate the need for a comprehensive yet entertaining introduction to these disciplines when I became involved with Economics-*Pennsylvania*, a nonprofit organization focusing on economics and investing education for K–12 students. Working with kids, creating experiences to help make saving and investing an integral part of their lives, has become a passion of mine.

As my work with students intensified, I realized that parents might also benefit from a fun investing primer. That became the principal inspiration for this book. For providing that inspiration, I'd like to express my most sincere appreciation to Fritz Heinemann, president and CEO of Economics*Pennsylvania*. Fritz and his wonderful kids have enabled me to see my professional field with fresh eyes; the view is nothing less than revelation.

I would also like to thank David B. Root, Jr. for his vision and encouragement at our firm, D.B. Root & Company. David has been my friend and mentor for 16 years. I've learned the meaning and value of service by observing David's work with our clients: always listening, always educating, and never assuming that we know more than they do. In fact, many of the questions in our IQ quiz were posed by our clientele. A big thanks to our clients for driving us to fill in the gaps in our own knowledge.

My colleagues at D.B. Root & Company were supportive of this endeavor. Special thanks to Lynne Hoffay, Arren Cyganovich, and Stacy Zatek for their participation in research and their patience with my bizarre schedule.

My daughter, Kelli, was a tremendous asset in the development of this book far beyond her willingness to share her computer. When the market turned bearish, she came home from school, plopped her books on the table, and asked, "When are stocks going to get better?"

I positively beamed with pride. My teenage daughter was taking a precocious interest in investing, in Mom's life.

"Because," she continued, "I'm tired of people always asking me what my mom thinks about the market." Oh well. It was a start, anyway, and it underscored the need for this book.

Finally, this project never could have clicked without my coauthor, Evan Pattak. His responsibilities are many—he researches, deciphers, assembles, prods—yet he is unflappable, even under extreme deadline pressure. Here's a piece of financial advice (at no charge): If you're thinking about writing a book, you'll do well to invest in a partner like Evan.

—Carrie Coghill

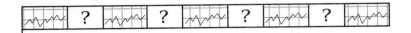

Contents

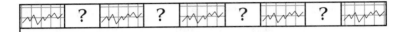

Introduction

Planning for a secure financial future never has been more challenging—or more rich with opportunity. Not only are people living longer, requiring larger retirement nest eggs, but investment vehicles have become more numerous and complex. Mention such terms as "P/E ratio," "derivatives," and "back-end loads" to most people and you'll likely get blank looks in return.

There's plenty of information available, but much of that information comes with baggage. Financial institutions, periodicals, and investor Websites typically have products or services to sell, making it difficult for consumers to evaluate advice from such sources. A program of research and study could help most people sort through the "investo-babble," but that regimen is too strict for most.

Thus, there's a real danger that folks who could take advantage of sophisticated financial planning strategies will never investigate them, out of fear of their complexity. If you're in that group, *What's Your Investing IQ?* was written with you in mind.

We've tried to produce a fun, educational tool—written in everyday language with a minimum of jargon—to help familiarize you with investing. *IQ* covers all the basics of investing: approaches, institutions, options, risks, and costs.

Each chapter includes multiple-choice questions about investing, finance, and economics, with hypothetical points awarded for each correct answer. The real learning will occur in the answers, which provide definitions, historical perspective, and suggestions on how financial vehicles can best be deployed. As you take the quiz, you're invited to tally your score on the forms provided and keep a running total. At the book's end, you'll have your final score...and you'll know where you stand on the Investing IQ Scale.

We begin *IQ* with a look at some of the bedrock institutions of investing, including stock markets—both domestic and foreign—and stock exchanges. Our next few series of questions deal with your understanding of asset classes, and how investing in multiple asset classes can diversify your portfolio and enhance your return. We probe your knowledge of the two broadest approaches to markets—speculating and investing—and how macroeconomic forces affect each.

IQ tests your familiarity with individual asset selection and the various types of risk associated with each asset class, along with your grasp of some of the more exotic investment possibilities. You'll also be quizzed on your awareness of the tax consequences of investing. Finally, we'll find out what you know about monitoring and adjusting your portfolio—and what's involved with hiring someone for advice in those areas.

Underlying all our questions and answers are two broad themes. The first is that investing involves both *careful study of all the options* and the *determination to pursue long-term growth* rather than chasing the elusive quick score. Our second important motif is that, if long-range prosperity is your chief investment goal, you're most likely to achieve it with a *diversified portfolio that minimizes your risk.* If you come away from *IQ* sharing our convictions in these two fundamental regards, we'll have done our job in preparing you.

We expect that novice investors can be the biggest beneficiaries of *IQ*. If you're in this group, our book won't tell you everything you need to know—no single volume does. But it should introduce you to some key concepts and reveal any gaps in your knowledge and experience.

Veteran investors may profit from *IQ* as well. If you've followed the same investment practices for many years, you may be on autopilot, operating on inertia rather than from an updated information base. *IQ* can remind you why you're doing what you're doing and help you kick any bad habits developed over the years.

Finally, if you're an investment professional, we'd like to suggest that *IQ* will be useful to you as well. You'll ace the quiz, no doubt about that. But the questions can help reintroduce your clients' most basic needs and fears, and enable you to deal with those in straightforward ways.

Have fun with the quiz. Find out what you know...and what you still need to know. That's a good starting point for any investor.

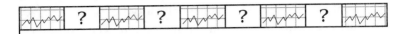

1 Goal Setting—
Too Thin, Maybe, but Never Too Rich

Financial security is everyone's goal, but how secure is secure? For some, security means having enough money to pay the monthly bills and maybe a little "mad money" left over. For others, security is an unending quest, the grail of a financial cushion big enough to soften even the harshest economic blows. Whatever your definition of security, today's economy can make its pursuit a frustrating adventure.

Above all, we live in an era of dislocation. Think, even for a minute, that your career is on the fast track, and your company hits a speed bump and downsizes. Consider your family finances secure and a loved one suffers a debilitating and costly illness that could eat up your entire savings.

And how about the prospect of long-term care for you and your spouse, to say nothing of your parents'? How many of us are secure enough to cover those bills? We know a couple who saved enough money to finance long-term care insurance, only to be forced to reallocate their savings to care for their terminally ill dog. Alas, nature took its course with the dog, while the couple is as financially insecure as ever.

13

It's often said that you can never be too thin or too rich. As any physician can tell you, you *can* be too thin. But can you be too rich? Where money is concerned, it may seem that we never have enough. Yet if we define financial security as the state where you have adequate resources to cover your daily needs, underwrite your most treasured goals, and account for life's unexpected contingencies, then the quest can be finite. Financial security *is* possible.

We know that it won't happen from relying on earnings alone. The sad fact is that no matter how talented and diligent you are when working, your earnings never will reflect your performance. For better or worse, our society tends to reward risk—the risk of ownership—more handsomely than it does hard work. If that's the case, then the key to your financial security may lie in investing.

When you invest, you put your money to work in ways that don't require much of your time. Your money makes money, even while you continue to earn your salary, giving you a sort of "double-dipping" effect. And if you're able to let your money grow without tapping the proceeds, you'll realize a compounding effect—your money will grow exponentially rather than arithmetically.

This is *not* to diminish the risks associated with investing—these are real. People most likely to succeed at investing are those who understand all the key investment vehicles, those who have the best feel for the risks and rewards, and those who can minimize the former and maximize the latter.

Are you one of those people ready to achieve financial security through investing? Read on. We'll provide you with much of the background you need for successful investing, even as we test your current investing "IQ" through a series of fun questions. You'll know what you know—and what you still need to know to achieve financial security.

So forget about that fad diet and think about fattening your bank account. In the first chapter, we'll look at some investment fundamentals—not specific vehicles but the basic principles of financial management, such as goal development and modification. Our guess is that you will crush this first chapter—and be ready for stiffer challenges to your investment IQ.

Question 1—

Why is it important to have financial goals?

a) To understand the types of investments you should own.

b) To motivate you to save.

c) To identify how much money you need to save.

d) To discourage you from saving because your goals are unattainable.

The best answer: c) To identify how much money you need to save.

The first step in any financial plan is establishing goals. What will your goals be? Saving for a home? Putting your kids through college? Early retirement? Most of us dream of these goals and more. If we identify our goals, we can put price tags on them. We'll know how much money it will take (and how much we must save) to achieve our goals. Without clearly defined goals, we may make poor investment decisions. Without goals, we're like motorists without a destination. Even with the best road map, we get no closer to completing our journey, because we don't know *where* we're going. Investing requires the same realization—without goals, you may be spinning your wheels.

Consider how goals (or lack thereof) can affect your approach to the stock market. Broadly speaking, the stock market can be used in two ways: for speculating or for investing. Speculating is akin to gambling, the lust for a quick buck. We saw speculation at a white-hot fever during the Internet and technology craze of the late 1990s. Everyone wanted in on the next "can't-miss" tech start-up; few paid attention to the fundamentals of the market, and they paid the price when the dotcoms dot went. There were a few winners, but many more losers. What these investors lacked were clearly defined long-term goals.

But the stock market can be used as an investment tool as well. To do so, you study the fundamentals and develop certain expectations of risk and return, and you invest accordingly. Past performance is no indication of future results, of course, but it can help identify what levels of risk have been associated with various investment sectors. And you'll eliminate emotion and speculation from the equation.

The most difficult aspect of the market is dealing with its fluctuations. Typically, our emotions take over and lead us to ill-considered decisions. During the '90s boom, for example, even someone with a sound strategy may have been seduced by highly speculative investments, succumbing to the emotion of greed. On the flip side, during the market decline that began in 2000—especially after the devastating events of 9/11—droves of investors abandoned their sound long-term strategies. They yielded to emotion just as unhesitatingly as the go-go crowd of the '90s. This time, the emotion in charge was fear rather than greed.

As accounting scandals extended the market's woes through the summer of 2002, investors were more uncertain than ever and fled the market. What many failed to consider was that legislation to rein in wayward CEOs, accountants, and auditors would help to restore investor confidence and turn the market around. If you have the foresight to anticipate such corrective actions, you'll trump fear and greed and survive the challenging times.

The market is amazingly true to its fundamentals over reasonable periods of time, say, 10 to 15 years. Although the events that precipitate greed, fear, and other emotional responses may change, the fundamentals of the market prevail. If you don't know what your investment goals are, you're prey to emotional decisions. But if you know your goals and maintain confidence in them, you'll stay focused on your investment objectives and time lines.

If you answered a)To understand the types of investments you should own, you score points as well. Once you establish your goals, you'll be well-positioned to determine what investment vehicles you should own and how much to invest in each. Let's say you identify early retirement as your main objective—you'd like to hang 'em up before age 59 1/2. If you sock all your money into a 401(k) plan or an IRA—which generally are wonderful savings vehicles—you may find that you can't get access to your money before age 59 1/2 without paying substantial penalties. Since you know your goal, you'll explore savings vehicles in addition to IRAs and 401(k) plans so that you have painless access to your money when you retire.

Let's clarify what we mean by *investment vehicles* and *investment sectors*. If we go back to our automobile analogy, selecting investment vehicles is comparable to choosing a car. With automobiles, your goals determine your selection. If you have a family, you may need a sturdy mini-van; if you're single or don't have children, a spiffy two-seater sports car may be right for you. Only after you make the fundamental vehicle choice are you ready to look at such options as color, AC, wet bar, the whole works.

As in automobile selection, investment selections are based on your goals. As noted, if you're saving for retirement, the best vehicles may be a 401(k) plan, an IRA, or an annuity. If college education is your priority, appropriate vehicles would be a 529 college savings account, a Coverdell IRA, or a custodial account. Now that you have the vehicles, you're ready for the options—investment sectors, including stocks and bonds. It's a sequential thing: first come the vehicles, then the sectors.

Many investment vehicles are tailored to specific goals. For example, 401(k) plans allow you to save "before tax" money while your account grows on a tax-deferred basis—an excellent retirement planning tool. Investment sectors, with their varying degrees of risk, can function in the same way. Some fluctuate more than others on an annual basis. Typically, it will be those sectors with varying risks that offer you the greatest return potential over the long term.

Therefore, your time line for achieving your goals becomes a driving factor in the risk you can tolerate. If you know the stock market has the potential to plummet in any given year, then it probably isn't a great investment sector for the cash you've earmarked for the purchase of a home next year. But as Figure 1-1 illustrates, stocks can offer the richest upside potential over lengthy periods. The chart is based on performance from 1926 to 2001 of large-company stocks, long-term corporate bonds, and T-Bills.

	Investment Sector Performance					
Holding Period (years)	**Investment Sector**					
	Stocks		**Bonds**		**Treasury Bills**	
	Best %	Worst %	Best %	Worst %	Best %	Worst %
1	53.99	-43.34	42.56	-8.09	14.71	-0.02
5	23.92	-12.47	22.51	-2.22	11.12	0.07
10	20.06	-0.89	16.32	0.98	9.17	0.15
15	18.24	0.64	13.66	1.02	8.32	0.22

Figure 1-1. Investment Sector Performance.

If you create a plan and stick to it, you'll avoid emotional investing responses. When the market soars, you won't get greedy and buy into highly speculative start-ups; when the market tanks, you won't give in to fear and bail out. Once you've identified your goals and understand how to invest your money, you'll be motivated to stick with your plan. Just knowing that you'll be able to accomplish your goals will be a huge inspiration. So, if your answer was b), you get points.

If you answered d) because your goals seem as unattainable as walking on the moon, it's way too early in the game to be frustrated. There are several steps you can take. Revisit your budget to identify additional savings opportunities. Get more aggressive with your investments. Figure 1-2 demonstrates how dramatically your savings will grow if you improve your average annual return through more aggressive investing.

Impact of Investment Returns		
	2% Total Return	**8% Total Return**
Monthly Savings	$50	$50
Number of Years	30	30
Future Value	$24,636	$74,518

Figure 1-2. Investment Returns.

Putting all your excess money in a savings account at the bank? Think about reallocating your money to a growth-oriented mutual fund. That will be one small step for you, but a giant leap toward the realization of your goals.

Scoring:

Give yourself 3 points for a), 2 points for b), 4 points for c). No points for d), but keep at it. You'll have plenty of chances to catch up.

Question 2—

In establishing your goals, which of these measures is essential in calculating how much money you need to save?

a) Inflation rate.

b) Number of years to reach your goal.

c) Expected rate of return on investments.

d) All of the above.

As you determine your goals, you need to know a number of things—how many years you have to reach your objectives, the projected after-tax returns on your investments, and the inflation rate, both generally and in relation to your specific goals. So, the best answer here is d) All of the above.

Let's look at this principle in action and imagine that you're saving for college education, and that your child currently is 3 years old. Let's further suppose that you want to send junior to a private college—nothing but the best for your kid, right?—that today costs $20,000 annually. Here's how you apply the three key calculation factors:

We'll first *consider the specific inflation in college costs*; these have been rising at the rate of approximately 6 percent per year. Therefore, to arrive at the costs for you, you'll need to inflate today's $20,000 cost by 6 percent per year until your child is finished with college. When you run the numbers this way, your costs for each of the four collegiate years will be $47,931, $50,807, $53,885, and $57,087. Your total costs for college will be a tidy $209,710.

Scary, isn't it? Many times, people forget to apply the inflation rate to their goals. Even when they do, they tend to disbelieve the figures because they are so god-awful. That's the impact inflation can have on our lives.

Now you know how much money you need, and *how long you have to produce it*—the second of our three calculation factors. The third step is to *determine how much you need to save*. This is done by looking at your present assets and projecting their growth based on the likely after-tax return of your investments.

This is the subjective element in the mix; we simply don't know what stocks or bonds will yield over the next 15 years. But we can use historical performance to plug in some reasonable growth figures. The key is to consider long-term results and not be swayed by short-term swings that may be aberrant. The value of your stocks may have jumped 30 percent in a boom year, but it's unreasonable and dangerous to project that as your average annual return. Long-term results will account for the ups and downs of business cycles and level out the peaks and valleys. Figures 1-3a (page 22), 1-3b (page 23), and 1-3c (page 24) will help you apply the three calculation factors to your goals and determine how much you need to save each year.

Scoring:
Score 4 points for d), 1 point for a), b), or c).

Here's a quick and useful way of determining what you need to save to reach your goal, whether it be retirement, college education, or a new home.

Saving for Your Goals

1. Amount Required for Goal (today's dollars) $_____

2. Number of Years Available for Saving   _____

3. Inflation Multiplier (from chart)   x_____

4. Future Value of Amount Required (multiply amount required by infaltion multiplier) $_____

5. Annual Payment Divisor (from chart)   _____

6. Annual Savings Required to Meet Goal (divide future value of amount required by annual payment divisor) $_____

Line 1: Enter the amount you need for your goal.

Line 2: Enter the number of years available until you need your money.

Line 3: Go to Fig. 1-3b and find the number under "Years to Goal" that matches the number you entered on Line 2. Move across to the expected rate of inflation. Enter this number on Line 3.

Line 4: Multiply the number from Line 1 by the number from Line 3 and enter the result here. This represents the total amount you need to save.

Line 5: Go to Fig. 1-3c and find the number under "Years to Goal" that matches the number you entered on Line 2. Move across to the expected annual rate of return for your investments. Enter this number on Line 5.

Line 6: Divide the number from Line 4 by the number from Line 5. Enter the result here. This is what you must save each year to meet your goal.

Figure 1-3a. Goal Worksheet.

Inflation Multiplier		
	Inflation Rate	
Years to Goal	**3%**	**4%**
1	1.030	1.040
2	1.061	1.082
3	1.093	1.125
4	1.126	1.170
5	1.159	1.217
6	1.194	1.265
7	1.230	1.316
8	1.268	1.369
9	1.305	1.423
10	1.344	1.480
11	1.384	1.539
12	1.426	1.601
13	1.469	1.665
14	1.513	1.732
15	1.558	1.801
16	1.605	1.873
17	1.653	1.948
18	1.702	20.26
19	1.754	2.107
20	1.806	2.191

Identify your inflation multiplier by going to the row that represents the number of years available for savings and moving across to the expected rate of inflation.
This chart is for illustration purposes only. The actual rate of inflation may vary.

Figure 1-3b. Inflation Multiplier.

Annual Payment Divisor		
Years to Goal	**6%**	**8%**	**10%**
1	1.000	1.000	1.000
2	2.060	2.080	2.100
3	3.184	3.246	3.310
4	4.375	4.506	4.641
5	5.637	5.867	6.105
6	6.975	7.336	7.716
7	8.394	8.923	9.487
8	10.897	10.637	11.436
9	11.491	12.488	13.579
10	13.181	14.487	15.937
11	14.972	16.645	18.531
12	16.870	18.977	21.384
13	18.882	21.495	24.523
14	21.015	24.215	27.975
15	23.276	27.152	31.772
16	25.673	30.324	35.950
17	28.213	33.750	40.545
18	30.906	37.450	45.599
19	33.760	41.466	51.159
20	36.786	45.762	57.275

Identify your annual savings divisor by going to the row that represents the number of years available for savings and move across to your expected annual return on savings.
This chart is for illustration purposes only. Your actual rate of return may vary.

Figure 1-3c. Annual Payment Divisor.

Question 3—

Which of the following can have the most surprising impact on your ability to reach your goals?

a) Investment returns.

b) Changes in tax laws.

c) How consistently you're saving for your goals.

d) Changing the timing of your goals.

The slightest change in investment returns can have a huge impact on your goals—especially when those goals are for the long term. So, the best answer here is a) Investment returns.

Most people don't realize how seemingly slight variances in investment returns can upset their financial apple carts. To demonstrate this, let's assume you're planning for retirement in 30 years, and you want to accumulate $1 million by Golden Watch Day. (In today's economy, by the way, this is not an unreasonable comfort zone.)

If you assume a 10 percent rate of return on investments, you'll need to save approximately $442 each month to reach your goal. If you miss your targeted investment return and earn an average of 9 percent annually, you'll accumulate $809,000—nearly $200,000 less than your goal, representing a shortfall of 20 percent!

That's why it's so important to be conservative with your projected investment returns. Remember, returns average out over long periods of time. Once you know that equity investments have provided an average return of about 10 percent over the past 25 years, it would be a mistake to think that your portfolio will continue to earn 20 percent after a boom year—and forego additional savings contributions as a result. Seasoned investors realize that at some point, they'll be giving some of that return back.

The same philosophy applies on the downside. When the market slides, some question whether this "investing stuff" really works. Such doubts were widespread during our most recent market slump. But two years—even three or four—don't constitute the long term. Interestingly, the beginning of the 20th century brought a market skid that was repeated almost exactly 100 years later. Investors recovered then, and they will again. The market tends to reward investors who stay the course; over time, it usually provides enough upside to make up for the downswings.

Some market gurus teach that understanding financial statements, economic trends, and ratios are the most difficult aspects of investing. Yet these are technical skills that can be acquired in relatively short order. In our experience, controlling fear and greed are the keys to successful investing. The best control is information—understanding how your investments have performed in recent years and over the long term. When you realize that your investments will compensate over time for any recent negative performance, you won't feel any pressure to overreact.

If you answered b), c), or d), you score points as well. Changes in tax laws clearly will influence your ability to reach your goals because they affect your return on investment. (When you project your investment returns, remember to use the "after-tax" returns. "Before-tax" projections are at best, useless, at worst, useless and deceptive.)

Consider these examples: If you own stock and sell it for a profit, you're now liable for the capital gains tax, which will reduce your return on this investment. If the value of your stock appreciated 10 percent but you owe a capital gains tax of 20 percent, guess what? Your after-tax return is now 8 percent,

0319726

not the 10 percent appreciation you thought you realized. If you don't factor in the after-tax figure, your financial plan could come up short. The point to remember here is that *prior to a 1997 tax law change, capital gains were taxed at a maximum rate of 28 percent.* Using this same example, the after-tax return would have been 7.8 percent under the old law. Therefore, this tax law modification of 1997 helped investors.

Another important change in tax law occurred with the Economic Growth and Tax Relief Reconciliation Act of 2001, which increased the annual limit on Individual Retirement Account (IRA) contributions from $2,000 to $3,000. Because IRAs allow for tax-free or tax-deferred growth (depending on which type you qualify for and utilize) you'd be crazy not to exploit them. Contributing to them year after year allows your money to grow—without generating immediate taxes.

Figure 1.4 on page 28 shows how advantageous IRAs can be; they became even more attractive with the new rules. Our projections compare the growth of the maximum-allowed IRA contributions for the next 30 years ($3,000 in 2003-2004; $4,000 in 2005-2007; $5,000 thereafter) invested on a tax-deferred versus taxable basis. We assume a 10 percent average annual return on that investment and average annual taxes of 20 percent if the taxable route were chosen. As the figure shows, in this scenario, your IRA account would grow to $793,884, while the total for taxable investments would be $546,721. The tax-deferral feature of IRAs results in a nest egg that's more than 45 percent richer—a huge difference.

Tax laws are in a constant state of flux. The 2001 act alone brought more than 400 changes to the federal tax code. It's imperative to understand how tax law changes affect your investment returns. Also, pay attention to the changes that legislators—and candidates for office—are proposing, and vote accordingly. Whatever you save in taxes can be invested in your future.

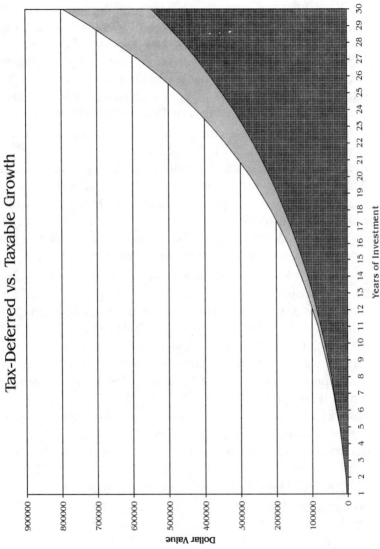

Figure 1-4.
Tax-
Deferred vs.
Taxable
Growth.

As for answer c), inconsistency in your savings pattern can derail your goals. Your initial calculation of the savings you'll require to meet your goals depends on the frequency of your contributions to savings. But if you omit one of your scheduled savings contributions—even with the intention of doubling up later—the investment period is shorter, your ultimate return smaller. The "double up" is really a double cross.

Finally, if you change the original time line for accomplishment of your goals, you also may be changing your ability to get there. If, for example, you decide to advance your retirement by five years, your savings needs can increase dramatically.

Goal modification is not always a bad thing, and it's inevitable in any case. If you have two children and learn that number three is on the way, you'll likely need to rethink your education needs and retirement objective. Buying a large home with an outrageous mortgage payment can have the same effect, while working hard and receiving a year-end bonus can facilitate earlier retirement. In our financial lives, trade-offs are part of the game.

Scoring:
Score 4 points for a), 3 for b), 2 for c), 1 for d).

Question 4—
How frequently should you review your financial plan and goals?

a) Semiannually.

b) Annually.

c) Every two years.

d) Every five years.

In financial planning and investing, change is constant. Tax laws change just about every year, sometimes cosmetically, sometimes dramatically. Your personal situation changes with each promotion, new job, or relocation. Because change is constant, your response to change must be just as regular. Reviewing your investment portfolio semiannually may be the most effective way to achieve financial consistency.

Annual reviews aren't frequent enough. If you review your portfolio and financial goals only once a year, you may not have enough time to adjust to the specific tax law changes for that year. Every two years is worse, every five years unthinkable.

Reviewing your holdings and game plan twice each year doesn't imply that changes are required that frequently. But you'll be establishing a discipline that will position you to make modifications when they are needed...and bring you peace of mind as well.

One warning here: As you review, don't overreact to the recent performance of your investments. Investment sectors come in and out of favor. If something you own has slipped over the past six months, don't dump it just because of softness in that sector. If other investments of the same type have done well while yours have floundered, then it may be time to question the investment...and undertake additional research

Scoring:

Score 4 points for a), 2 for b), 1 for c), 0 for d).

	Scoring for Chapter 1	
	Highest Possible Score	**Your Score**
Question 1	4	_____
Question 2	4	_____
Question 3	4	_____
Question 4	4	_____
CHAPTER TOTALS	16	_____

2 Investment Vehicles— Baby, You Can Drive These Cars

The world of investing can be as bewildering as it is exciting. While there always have been plenty of investment options available, many of these were long regarded as obscure, province of professional money managers only. Now, thanks in part to the dot-com boom of the late '90s that brought unprecedented discretionary income into play, investments once considered exotic are now commonly discussed—and sometimes selected. This gives you a tremendous range of investment options but also much more to ponder and research than ever before.

We've gone well beyond stocks and bonds as investment sectors. In stocks, we can consider Small Cap (market capitalization less than $1 billion), Mid Cap (market capitalization between $1 billion and $5 billion), and Large Cap (market capitalization greater than $5 billion) companies; domestic- and foreign-based firms; small technology enterprises that focus on growth rather than dividends; old, reliable institutions—the so-called Blue Chips—that produce moderate growth but regular dividends; long or short positions in any or all of the above.

With bonds, we're able to choose from corporate, government, or municipal sectors, scope out the most attractive returns and maturity periods, and decide whether taxable or tax-free bonds suit us best.

The issues become even more complex when we're thinking of these sectors as components of a mutual fund or other investment account. Do the same principles of selection apply when our stocks and bonds are part of mutual funds, individual retirement accounts, or 401(k) plans? Where do annuities fit in the picture, if at all? Should we be looking at growth funds, income funds, or both? Are investment funds that feature foreign-based companies a good idea?

Clearly, we have much to consider in selecting our investment vehicles. In making their choices, many investors look only at the potential return; that's often difficult enough to gauge, but it also leaves out some key variables in determining the best investment vehicles for you. Specifically, it's vital to consider these three features of any potential investments:

- ▣ Tax consequences.

- ▣ Accessibility.

- ▣ Distribution to your heirs upon your death.

Because people tend to overlook these investment characteristics, sometimes with serious consequences, our questions in this chapter will probe your knowledge of these key features. Once you understand the implications of these features, you'll be prepared to drive your investment vehicles all the way to financial security.

Question 1—

Which of the following investment vehicles will transfer through your estate according to your will?

a) Assets titled in individual name.

b) Assets titled in joint name with rights of survivorship.

c) Assets owned in "transfer on death accounts."

d) Assets owned in an IRA.

This question really is about titling, that is, the name or names in which assets are held. Only assets held in individual name—your name only—will transfer directly through your will at your death, so the correct answer here is a). How your assets are titled can have a great bearing on your control of those assets and your ability to direct them to the heirs you've selected, so titling is a topic that merits some discussion.

As noted, one titling option for your assets is to hold them in individual name. This option provides you with the greatest amount of control while you're alive. You are the sole owner of assets listed in individual name and need no approval or authorization from anyone if you wish to sell or distribute the assets. Typically, assets held in individual names are taxable. So if you're in a high-income tax bracket, you should pay attention to the amount of taxable income and capital gains that your individually titled assets are generating. And if you're holding these assets to accumulate money to finance retirement or college education, perhaps you'd be better off with tax-deferred or tax-free vehicles.

If you hold assets in individual name, you must consider two vital points. First, who will manage these assets if you become ill or incapacitated and cannot handle your own financial affairs? When assets are owned in individual name, no one, except you, has access to them...not your spouse, not your parents or children, not your golfing buddies. So, if you think your spouse or sibling automatically will take over your finances if you're unable to manage them, you're courting disaster.

The solution: Create power-of-attorney documents that specify who will act on your behalf in times of emergency, illness, accident, or incapacity. The documents not only name a trustee, but they also itemize the authority of the trustee. Absent such documents, your loved ones must go to court, leaving selection of a trustee to the discretion of a judge...and your estate in a mess for months.

Just as important is the second point: you'll need a will to distribute individually titled assets to your heirs as you see fit. If you die "intestate" (that is, without a will), the courts will make your distribution decisions for you according to your state's intestacy laws. These determine the pecking order for distribution of your assets. Typically, your spouse and children will be the first beneficiaries, then parents, then siblings, and so on down the line. In many cases, the lineup is not what you would have chosen had you been around to make the call. You can avoid this unfortunate situation by creating a will.

Remember, titling and beneficiary designations take precedence over your will. The only assets you can bequeath through your will are those you own individually—and haven't directed via a beneficiary designation.

As we've seen, titling your assets individually brings both advantages and concerns. The same can be said of the other principal option: joint titling. There are several variations. **Assets held in joint name with rights of survivorship** automatically transfer to your joint owner at the time of your death. This happens regardless of any stipulations in your will; titling takes precedence over the will. These assets will pass to the ultimate heirs via your joint owner's will at his or her death.

Another titling option is **joint tenants in common.** In this structure, each joint tenant is assigned a percentage of the asset. Although these assets function as joint accounts, either tenant may sell his or her portion without authorization of the other tenant. At death, the assigned percentage of the decedent's portfolio becomes part of the estate and is distributed to heirs via the will, through the probate process.

In certain states and with certain property, you also may opt for the titling option known as **joint tenants by the entirety.** The advantage of this approach is that it designates the asset as "entirely" belonging to each tenant. Thus, it offers protection for assets as long as both tenants are living. Creditors can seize the assets *only* if the nonindebted spouse dies first. Should the indebted spouse die first, the assets pass automatically to the surviving spouse; there are no assets remaining for creditors to grab.

Be wary of establishing this type of joint tenancy solely to shield your assets from a legal judgment or settlement. If a court sniffs out that ploy, it could strike down the transfer, leaving your wealth as exposed as before and giving you a black eye in that court.

Finally, consider the option known as **transfer on death accounts**, which are offered in all states, and can be deployed for assets titled individually, assets titled to joint tenants with rights of survivorship, and assets titled to joint tenants by entirety. With the aid of a financial institution, you establish an account that allows you to designate heirs for the underlying assets; probate is avoided, and the transfer of assets to your heirs goes smoothly.

There's an important caveat with transfer on death accounts. In the case of assets titled to joint tenants with rights of survivorship, those assets pass to the ultimate heirs only upon the second tenant's death. In the intervening period between the death of the parties, the designation of beneficiary is subject to change. A will or trust may provide more security and flexibility than this type of account. Avoiding probate is nice, but not at the expense of your assets ending up somewhere you wouldn't have wanted them.

In this discussion of titling, we would be remiss if we didn't consider IRAs, one of the most popular savings vehicles. They come in multiple varieties, but no matter the type of IRA, it must be individually titled. Assets within IRAs are transferred to your heirs by beneficiary designation. If no beneficiary is named, the assets flow into your estate and are distributed via the will—which may bring negative tax consequences. That brings us to our next question.

Scoring:
Score 4 points for a), 0 for any other answer.

Question 2—

Which of the following IRAs has the fewest eligibility restrictions?

a) Roth IRA.

b) Non-deductible IRA.

c) Traditional IRA.

d) Spousal IRA.

Of all IRAs, non-deductible IRAs impose the fewest eligibility requirements, so the correct answer is b). The catch, of course, is that the benefits for this type of IRA may be less generous than those offered by other IRAs. The only significant eligibility rule: Your earned income in a given year must at least equal your contribution that year. With non-deductible IRAs, your account grows on a tax-deferred, rather than tax-free, basis. Withdrawals are mandatory once you reach age 70 1/2 and are based upon the uniform required minimum distribution (RMD) table.

The IRS insists on minimum distributions so that it can begin to collect income tax on your account. RMD rules long have been a source of confusion, but the calculation has become much easier over the past few years. You can determine your RMD by dividing your account balance on December 31 of the previous year by your life expectancy, as indicated in Figure 2-1.

IRS Uniform Required Minimum Distribution Table			
Age	**Divisor**	**Age**	**Divisor**
70	26.2	85	13.8
71	25.3	86	13.1
72	24.4	87	12.4
73	23.5	88	11.8
74	22.7	89	11.1
75	21.8	90	10.5
76	20.9	91	9.9
77	20.1	92	9.4
78	19.2	93	8.8
79	18.4	94	8.3
80	17.6	95	7.8
81	16.8	96	7.3
82	16.0	97	6.9
83	15.3	98	6.5
84	14.5	99	6.1

Figure 2-1. RMD Table.

For example, if you turn 70 1/2 in 2003, divide your account balance on December 31, 2002, by 26.2. The result is your RMD—with one interesting exception. If the sole beneficiary of your account is more than 10 years younger than you, you can base your distributions on your "joint life expectancy." This would decrease your RMD as well as the taxes due. Remember that your required minimum distribution is just that—a minimum. You're free to withdraw more than the minimum.

For withdrawals from a non-deductible IRA prior to age 59 1/2, you'll incur taxes and a 10 percent penalty—but only on the earnings in your account. Whether you're making contributions or early withdrawals, you'll need to fill out IRS Form 8606 and submit it with your income tax return.

With other types of IRA, the requirements and benefits vary. Roth IRAs provide more flexible eligibility limitations than traditional IRAs. Although money contributed to a Roth IRA is not tax-deductible, the account grows tax-free. Even if you participate in a company-sponsored retirement plan, you're still eligible for a Roth IRA as long as you meet income eligibility requirements. As of 2002, if you're an individual tax filer, you can make a full Roth IRA contribution if your income is less than $95,000. Eligibility begins to phase out at $95,000 in income and ends when your income reaches $110,000. For couples filing jointly, a full contribution is permitted if the joint income is less than $150,000, with phase-out, meaning that the benefit diminishes—and ultimately disappears—as income rises, occurring between $150,000 and $160,000 in income.

If you withdraw money from your Roth IRA, it's tax-free as long as it comes from contributions. Distributions from earnings are tax-free when the owner has had the Roth IRA for five years AND:

▣ The owner is at least 59 1/2.

▣ The owner has died.

- ▣ The owner becomes disabled.

- ▣ The money is used for qualifying health insurance premiums or medical expenses.

- ▣ The money is part of a series of certain substantially equal payments.

- ▣ The money is used for qualified higher-education expenses.

or

- ▣ The money is used for first-time home-buying expenses for a qualifying family member ($10,000 lifetime cap).

A great feature of Roth IRAs is that you're never required to take distributions, at any age. Among IRAs, this characteristic is unique to the Roth IRA.

Traditional IRAs are tax-deductible, offer tax-deferred growth, and require minimum distributions at age 70 1/2, based on the RMD table in Fig. 2-1. However, the extent of your eligibility for traditional IRAs depends upon the availability of company-sponsored retirement plans where you work.

If you're eligible to participate in an employer retirement plan, the tax deductibility of your IRA contribution is reduced or eliminated depending on your modified adjusted gross income. Contributions are fully tax-deductible for single filers up to $34,000 of income (phase-out between $34,000 and $44,000); if you're married filing jointly, contributions are fully tax-deductible up to $54,000 of income (phase-out between $54,000 and $64,000). If you're not covered by a retirement plan but your spouse is (and you file jointly), tax deductibility depends on a different set of numbers. Your contribution is fully tax-deductible below $150,000 of income (phase-out between $150,000 and $160,000).

Spousal IRAs can be structured as Roth, traditional, or non-deductible. They allow for spouses to contribute to an IRA, even if they don't have earned income. Therefore, as long as the other spouse has earned enough income to cover both contributions and all other eligibility requirements are met, the spouse without earned income can maintain an IRA.

As we've seen, IRAs vary, but they have some common features. Withdrawals from any IRA prior to age 59 1/2 are subject to taxes and penalty, with some exceptions—these include withdrawals prompted by hardship or disability. Maximum contributions for all IRAs have been set by Congress as follows:

Year	Maximum IRA Contribution
2002	$3,000
2003	$3,000
2004	$3,000
2005	$4,000
2006	$4,000
2007	$4,000
2008	$5,000
2009+	Indexed for inflation

Also, there is an added benefit called a "catch-up feature" for those over 50 years old. If you're in that age bracket, you can add a catch-up contribution to your maximum contribution. Maximum catch-up increments by year are:

Year	Maximum "Catch-Up"
2002	$ 500
2003	$ 500
2004	$ 500
2005	$ 500
2006	$1,000
2007	$1,000
2008	$1,000
2009+	Indexed for inflation

IRAs are excellent savings vehicles, whether your account grows on a tax-free or tax-deferred basis. Which IRA is best for you? Consider our three key investment characteristics—tax consequences, accessibility, and distribution to your heirs—prioritize them for your needs, and you'll have the answer.

Scoring:
Score 4 points for b), 0 for any other answer.

Question 3—

With tax-deferred annuities, which is the most important consideration before purchase?

a) Your income tax rate.

b) The internal mortality and expense (M&E) costs and other surrender charges and commissions.

c) Investment options within the annuity.

d) Death benefit features.

Tax-deferred annuities, as the name suggests, are investment vehicles offered by life insurance companies that allow your earnings to accumulate, tax-deferred, until retirement. So no income taxes are due now on the income and capital gains your annuity generates. Sounds like a no-brainer, right? Actually, it's trickier than that.

Tax-deferred annuities were created as vehicles for a "guaranteed" income stream throughout retirement. In fact, the word *annuity* means payment of a fixed sum of money at regular intervals. At the time of annuitization (when payments begin), you may have the option of guaranteeing the payment over various time frames. For example, you can guarantee payment over your lifetime, over the remaining years of you and your spouse, or for some other specific period. If you lack a reliable retirement income stream, a tax-deferred annuity may be a great way to achieve some security. Structured properly, it's an income stream that you can't outlive. (However, when you opt for a guaranteed income stream, the insurance company typically becomes the principal of the annuity. The insurer may pay a death benefit to your beneficiaries upon your passing, but the balance belongs to the company.)

These vehicles come in two forms: *fixed* and *variable*. Fixed annuities offer a guaranteed rate of return for a certain period of time, with the return adjusted thereafter; even with the adjustment, a minimum interest rate typically is guaranteed. Variable annuities are basically mutual funds within an insurance policy; you get to pick from a wide range of mutual funds and families, enabling you to diversify your holdings. Whether you select a fixed or variable annuity is a product of your risk tolerance. Clearly, variable annuities bring greater risk than fixed annuities.

Annuities offer attractive death benefit features. If you die before the policy is annuitized, your beneficiaries typically will not receive less than the amount of money you put into the policy, minus any withdrawals you made. Other advantages: the amount of money you can invest is unlimited, and minimum withdrawals are not required, no matter your age.

That's an impressive roster of strengths, but there are negatives as well. First, when you withdraw money from your annuity, your earnings are taxed as ordinary income. Had your money been invested outside the annuity in a regular mutual fund account, your growth would have been considered capital gains and taxed at a lower rate than ordinary income.

In addition, annuities bring contract fees, administrative costs, and mortality expenses charged within the contract. The National Association for Variable Annuities indicates these expenses range from 1.5 percent to 2.0 percent on average.

Early withdrawals are another problem area. Before age 59 1/2, these will generate a 10 percent penalty from the IRS—as well as the taxes now due. If you need to reclaim some or all of your investment, you'll likely be hit with a *surrender charge*—imposed by the company that offers and administers your annuity—that can be as steep as 10 percent. Surrender charges typically decline over a number of years, often disappearing after 10 years. Many annuities permit limited withdrawals without surrender charges, but early withdrawals may still trigger income taxes and an IRS penalty.

A final potential negative: Because annuities are issued by private businesses, the "guarantee" that you think you're purchasing is only as strong as the stability of the issuing company. Should that company falter or fold, your "guaranteed" income stream will be guaranteed to give you a headache—and not much more.

Therefore, once you understand the advantages and disadvantages of tax-deferred annuities, perhaps the most important factors to consider before investing are your current income tax bracket and your projected bracket at retirement, making a) the best answer to this question. Remember that growth in your annuity will be taxed as ordinary income. If you project substantial growth from your annuity coupled with a high retirement-age tax rate, it could be that annuities are not the best vehicles for you. On the other hand, if you antici- pate a significant decline in your income once you retire—and a correspondingly lower tax rate—then annuities may be the way to go.

A little research will go a long way in evaluating annuities. Consider, for example, whether the tax-deferred growth will compensate for the fees associated with the annuity. Look also at the investment options within the plan. If it's a variable an- nuity, are you satisfied with the amount of diversification you'll be able to achieve? Once you've decided an annuity works from an income tax perspective, investment options within the plan become paramount.

Scoring:

Score 4 points for a). Because the other factors also are important, score 3 points for b), 2 for c), 1 for d).

Question 4—

Although all the following items are important in financial planning, which is the most critical in selecting investment vehicles?

a) Tax efficiency.

b) Ease of distribution to your heirs.

c) Access and availability of the asset.

d) Administrative expenses.

Success in financial planning requires, more than anything else, a resolute focus on basic priorities...and avoiding seductive but dangerous distractions. During the boom of the late 1990s, many investors were lured by the sirens' song—the lyrics were something like: *More money now!* All too often, these investors ran aground because they didn't stay true to their purpose. The quest became all about making as much money as possible without any consideration of costs, risk, personal and familial priorities, and taxes.

Be wary of hot new investment trends. Trends come and go, but the markets have been around for more than 150 years. The same fundamentals that applied a century-and-a-half ago still apply today. When you hear a so-called expert intone that "It's different this time," you can be pretty sure it's *the same* this time...except for the names of the unsuspecting victims of the latest go-go craze.

What are the fundamental issues? First and foremost is your *time frame*. Will you need your savings in a year for a new car...or in 30 years to finance retirement? Will your money be available when you need it? Can you access it if you need it sooner than planned?

These are among the most important questions for your financial plan. Not only will the answers help get you where you want to go, but they'll enable you to match investment vehicles with your goals. There's no sense investing in a long-term, tax-deferred annuity if you're targeting the money for a new home in five years. Understanding your time frame will help you develop an efficient overall plan, so the best answer here is c).

The tax-efficiency of your investments may be next in importance. If you don't consider them, taxes will be the invisible hand in your pocket, frustrating you during all your attempts at saving. The earlier you begin accumulating assets in a tax-efficient manner, the more money you'll have to achieve your goals.

Next, consider the cost of each investment. Include commissions, direct fees, and internal administration charges. Read each prospectus carefully and ask plenty of questions if you don't find what you want in it. We tend to shrug off these costs because each such charge seems tiny of itself. But if you're nicked 0.5 percent here, 1 percent there, and 2 percent for something else, pretty soon you're talking real money. And even if total costs are small, that doesn't mean a competitive vehicle might not feature costs that are smaller still. Comparisons are always in order.

Finally, consider the options for distribution of your holdings to heirs...but don't overdo it. The first objective of financial planning is to ensure *your* security. Even though IRAs and annuities pass to your heirs via beneficiary designations rather than probate, it doesn't necessarily follow that you should invest all your money in those vehicles. Prioritize your own needs, then do the best you can to ensure efficient and easy transfer to your heirs.

Scoring:

Score 4 points for c), 3 for a), 2 for d), 1 for b).

⩘⩗	Scoring for Chapter 2	⩘⩗
	Highest Possible Score	**Your Score**
Question 1	4	_____
Question 2	4	_____
Question 3	4	_____
Question 4	4	_____
CHAPTER TOTALS	16	_____

3 The Mysteries of the Market—
Hint: NASDAQ Is Not a Middle Eastern Potentate

The term "stock market" may conjure up images of a supermarket to you, but that doesn't exactly get to the essence of this curious institution. When you think market, think in terms of a bazaar, a frenzied hugger-mugger of a market where buyers and sellers engage in fevered negotiations, and where nothing has intrinsic value but is judged instead on a *perception* of its value.

That, in a nutshell, is the stock market. Companies sell shares in themselves based on their own unverifiable estimates of what their businesses are worth. Analysts offer recommendations about those shares, based on equally unverifiable crunching of such factors as price/earnings multiples along with wistful reviews of management teams. Investors purchase or sell shares in those companies, based on analysts' recommendations and their own perceptions of each company's growth potential.

The operative word here is *perceptions*. None of it really exists except as a system of shared perceptions. To be sure, the principal trading venues for the stock market—the floors of the stock exchanges—are colorful, lively places. But these are the mechanics of the market, not really the market itself. That exists primarily in our minds.

The power of the market is very real and very important. It's the foundation for the creation and expansion of publicly held businesses throughout much of the world. It creates wealth for individual and institutional investors...and can deplete it just as quickly. As an individual investor, your decisions may be based largely on perceptions; the impact of those decisions is measured in dollars and your financial security.

How can you make the best market decisions? By acquiring and evaluating the best information. The connection between the market, in the macro sense, and how it relates to your individual portfolio will help you make decisions and discern which information is relative to your situation. Remember, much of what we see and hear is hype—no more than one person's bag of perceptions—but not necessarily true or germane.

Keep well-informed, avoid emotional decisions, and you have a chance to do well in this financial bazaar known as the stock market.

We'll begin this test of your market knowledge with a pair of softballs before we proceed to tougher stuff.

Question 1—

When the market is in a prolonged upswing, the animal it most commonly is likened to is:

a) Bull.

b) Boar.

c) Lion.

d) Spotted Hyena.

Scoring:

If you said a) bull, give yourself 1 point. This question is so ridiculously easy that if you answered anything other than a), subtract 2 points.

Question 2—

When the market is in a lengthy downturn, the animal it most commonly is likened to is:

a) Possum.

b) Sloth.

c) Bear.

d) Koala.

Scoring:

The same scoring applies here: Add 1 point for the correct answer, c), subtract 2 points for any other answer.

So much for the appetizer. Now you're ready for the main course.

Question 3—

Of the following indexes, which gives us the broadest indication of how the stock market is performing?

a) Dow Jones Industrial Average.

b) Dow Jones Transportation Index.

c) S&P 500 Index.

d) Wilshire 5000 Index.

The Wilshire 5000 (d) is the best answer because it clearly represents the broadest range of companies, tracking the returns of nearly every U.S.-based publicly held company. Even the *5000* in its name is an understatement, since the index has grown since its 1974 debut to include approximately 6,300 companies. While the Wilshire 5000 effectively portrays the activity of domestic stocks, it does not track the stock of any foreign-based firms.

The S&P 500 Index, created on March 4, 1957, is the second broadest—as the name implies, it tracks 500 stocks—followed by the Dow Jones Industrial Average and the Transports.

Some may find this ranking of answers surprising, since the Dow is part of the common audio background of our lives, the white noise of finance. Every day we hear: *The Dow is up 40, the Dow is down 20.* We may cheer when the Dow is up, shudder when it's down, but does it have any relevance to our investments? To understand that, we first must understand what these figures mean, and why other indexes may be more significant to us than the Dow.

Stock market indexes are designed to give investors an indication of how stocks, or a cluster of certain companies, are performing in the market. Certain indexes may attempt to represent publicly held companies as a whole, or they may try to be a representative slice of certain sectors. Thus, one could imagine a technology index, say, or an agricultural index, or an exporters index.

Now consider the Dow Jones Industrial Average. This index was created way back on May 26, 1896. Although it began with only 12 stocks, it expanded to 30 stocks by 1928. That's where it sits today. The 30 stocks in the Dow are major players in their industries. Occasionally, Dow Jones & Company modifies the index, eliminating some firms and adding others, to maintain the index as a broad representation of the companies and industries that keep our economy humming. In addition, if a Dow company is acquired, Dow Jones must reevaluate its status in the index group.

The index was designed as an "average" of the movement of the underlying companies. The value of the index at any time is computed by adding up the stock prices of each company in the index, then finding an average by dividing that number by the number of stocks in the index. Over time, the divisor has been adjusted to reflect stock splits.

That's useful as far as it goes. But the Dow is an unweighted index. Other indexes, such as the Wilshire 5000 and the S&P 500, are weighted based on a company's market capitalization, which is determined by multiplying the number of shares a company has outstanding by the price per share. Because the Dow is unweighted, the price movements of the stocks are simply averaged, causing the stocks with higher prices to have more impact on the index than lower-priced stock.

The Dow Jones Transportation Average is the oldest stock index, created in 1884 as the Dow Jones Rail Index. At that time, it was mainly comprised of railroads. In 1970, the index was changed to the "transportation average" to reflect the impact of transport modes other than railroad. The index includes 20 transportation companies. If you think of it as a sector-specific index, you'll find it useful.

Depending on your investment philosophy and the diversity of your portfolio, you should select an index or indexes to help guide you and provide benchmarks. Using benchmarks for portfolio management gives you insight as to how well your investments are performing relative to the overall market. Remember, the indexes we've listed here are just a sample of the many that are available. For example, if you're invested 70 percent in U.S. stocks and 30 percent in international stocks, a combined benchmark of 70 percent S&P 500 and 30 percent EAFE Index (an international index) would be necessary to truly compare your investments to the overall market.

Many investors make the mistake of not using an appropriate index to compare portfolio performance. As we've seen, the index quoted most frequently, the Dow Jones Industrial Average, is usually the worst choice for benchmark comparisons. A weighted average offers a much better comparison.

Using overall market comparisons can help point out inequities in your portfolio. If your portfolio isn't doing so well, yet its comparable index is, you may want to re-evaluate your specific holdings and figure out why they're underperforming the index. On the other hand, if the comparable indexes are performing just as poorly as your stocks are, it may be a reflection of cyclical changes in overall market conditions. In this case, you may own quality investments that have a good chance of recovering as overall market conditions improve.

The goal is to keep information in perspective. This will prevent an overreaction to dramatic news in the wrong index.

Scoring:

> The best answer, d), is worth 4 points. However, since the other indexes can be useful in the right situations, score 3 points for c), 2 points for a), 1 point for b).

Question 4—

Which of the following is the most popular composite index?

a) New York Stock Exchange Composite.

b) American Stock Exchange (AMEX) Composite.

c) NASDAQ.

d) EAFE.

This question probes your understanding of the differences between indexes such as the Dow, which include a select basket of stocks, and composite indexes such as NASDAQ (National Association of Securities Dealers Automated Quotations System), which measure all stocks listed on the exchange. Composite indexes typically are market value-weighted, that is, you calculate the value of the index by multiplying the number of shares outstanding by the current price. This keeps any stock's effect on the index relative to its overall value in the market. Therefore, the stocks that drive down a composite index may not be the same stocks that push the index to recovery.

With the Dow, you can be reasonably confident that long-term trends are reflected in the prices of the 30 Dow stocks. The same can't be said of composite indexes, where the performance of any single stock can be masked by the movement of the hundreds of companies that make up the composite. For example, if you own a NASDAQ stock, you may be unsettled when a spurt in the NASDAQ index doesn't carry your stock along with it. This will be a clear, if not painful, demonstration of the potentially weak correlation between a composite index and any stock within the index—especially if the stock is fundamentally unsound and needs more than a surging sector to carry it along.

All stock exchanges and their corresponding indexes have some common features. Each exchange, for example, maintains requirements that companies must satisfy before they can be listed. These cover such characteristics as shareholder equity, pre-tax income, number of shares to be distributed, minimum share price, trading volume, and earnings. From there, the differences between the exchanges and indexes may be more important than their similarities.

NASDAQ (National Association of Securities Dealers Automated Quotations System) is a high-speed computerized network for trading over-the-counter (OTC) stocks, that is, stocks not listed on any other exchange. The NASDAQ index measures all such stocks. Though relatively young—it started trading on February 8, 1971—NASDAQ has become the most popular composite index, making c) the best answer to Question 4.

Why is NASDAQ so popular? You can find the answer in the organization vision NASDAQ presents on its Website *(www.nasdaq.com)*: *To build the world's first truly global securities market...a worldwide market of markets built on a worldwide network of networks...linking pools of liquidity and connecting investors from all over the world...assuring the best possible price for securities at the lowest possible cost.*

It used to be that young companies, or those based on unproven technologies or global markets, were more or less forced to be listed OTC because they couldn't meet the stringent listing requirements of established exchanges. Today, those companies are the very source of much of the market's excitement and momentum—whether upward or downward—and a target for many young investors who find a match for their own enthusiasm and agenda. Inevitably, these investors are keen followers of NASDAQ and invest in NASDAQ companies.

How important has NASDAQ become? On October 26, 1999, the Dow Jones Industrial Average tapped Microsoft and Intel for inclusion in the Dow, the first and only time NASDAQ companies have been so selected. In January 1985, NASDAQ wrote a fine point on its vision by creating the NASDAQ 100 Index. Unlike its sister composite index, the newer index represents 100 of the largest nonfinancial stocks. Technology companies dominate this index.

The NYSE Composite Index (formally known as the New York Stock Exchange Composite Index) debuted on January 1, 1966, although it can trace its roots way back to the founding of the New York Stock Exchange in 1792. As with all composite indexes, this one is designed to provide investors with a way to measure the overall movement of a particular market. In this case, the market measured may be thought of as the "Blue Chip" sector—large, prominent companies with lengthy track records— since most industrial and financial giants are NYSE companies.

The official Website of NYSE, *www.nyse.com*, states that it aims to provide "the highest-quality and most cost-effective, self-regulated marketplace for the trading of financial instruments." In a twist on the standard mission, the exchange also tries to "serve as a forum for discussion of relevant national and international policy issues."

The American Stock Exchange Composite Index represents all trades conducted on the American Stock Exchange (AMEX). This exchange focuses on a wide variety of listed stocks, options, and exchange traded funds (ETFs), which are baskets of stocks that are designed to track certain indexes yet trade like single stocks. AMEX pioneered this type of security.

MSCI EAFE Index is shorthand for The Morgan Stanley Capital International Europe, Australia, and Far East Index. Thank goodness for the acronym! While this index includes over 1,000 companies in 20 countries from the stock markets of Europe, Australia, and the Far East, it is not a composite index of a marketplace. Rather, it's an unmanaged, market value-weighted index that serves as the benchmark for most international mutual funds.

Understanding the indexes and what they measure will help you make apples-to-apples comparisons. You wouldn't, for example, compare changes in the MSCI EAFE to NASDAQ activity; they're measuring different phenomena. You're more likely to succeed as an investor when you understand what you're tracking...and how it relates to your holdings.

Scoring:

Score 4 points for c), but give yourself partial credit for any other answer—all these indexes are important. Score 3 points for a), 2 for b), 1 for d).

 ## Question 5—

Regarding a 2-for-1 stock "split," which of the following statements is the most complete and accurate?

a) As an existing holder of the stock, your value stays the same.

b) You should buy the stock prior to the split because after the split, you'll have double the shares.

c) You should purchase the stock immediately following the stock split because the price is less expensive.

d) If you own the stock, you should sell prior to the split to get the higher price.

In a stock split, shareholders receive additional shares for each share they own, based on a formula determined by the company. For example, if you hold 100 shares of Anapanaconda, and the company announces a 2-for-1 split, you'll end up with 200 shares. Stocks can split 3 for 2, 2 for 1, 5 for 4, 3 for 1—just about any way the company would like.

There also are reverse splits to reduce the number of out-standing shares. In our previous example, a 1-for-2 reverse split in Anapanaconda would leave you with 50 shares rather than your original 100.

The key to understanding the impact of stock splits is to remember that the split brings a comparable reconfiguration of share price. If your 100 shares of Anapanaconda traded at $50 before the 2-for-1 split, they'll be worth $25 apiece after the split. The overall value of your holdings in this company, $5,000, is unaffected by the split.

Thus, the impact of splits is largely psychological. Companies implement splits to lower the share price to a level that may be more comfortable for investors, who typically prefer to buy round lots of stock—multiples of 100 shares, for example. If a split lowers the share price from $50 to $25, new investors might decide to up the original ante; they can get twice as many shares for the original investment they contemplated.

Companies also split their stocks to enhance liquidity in their securities. The more easily their stock trades, the more likely it is that buyers will find sellers and sellers will find buyers. Splits can also indicate a company's confidence in its own future.

These effects can be real, but they remain part of a perceptual package. The fact of the matter is that a stock split has no impact on the value of your holdings because the share price is adjusted proportionately. This is the one inviolable truth, and that makes answer a) the best response here.

Even though splits don't affect you immediately, they can lead to some play in share prices. Much of this occurs during the gap between the announcement of the split and the effective date—usually about four to six weeks when investors looking for an edge can influence the price (although typically across a narrow range). Throughout these gaps, I can count on clients calling me with split-related advice: *Let's buy Anapanaconda now because the announced split will drive the price up and we'll realize some nice gains. Let's wait until the momentum of the split pushes Anapanaconda up, then sell all our shares at a nice profit.*

For the record, we tracked the performance of stocks that split during the first quarter of 2002, and here's what we found: There were 36 such splits during the quarter. In 34 of those instances, or more than 94 percent of the time, the share price rose at some point between the split announcement date and the split effective date. The highest peak was realized by DeWolfe (ticker symbol DWL), which crested at $17.97, or 46.6 percent above its price on split announcement day.

This data lends some support to the notion that you can jump into a stock after a split announcement and realize a quick profit. But there's more to the story than that. In 14 cases (38.9 percent), the stock price not only declined from its high, but it actually fell back *below* the share price on announcement day. Consider Movie Gallery (MOVI), which was trading at $17.33 on December 3, 2001, when it announced its split. Two days later, share price was up to $18.93. But by the time the split effective date of January 4, 2002, rolled around, the price had sunk to $14.76—14.8 percent *below* the price on announcement day. Sure, you could have realized a handsome gain by getting into Movie Gallery on December 3 and getting out on December 5, but who can time the market that precisely?

Moreover, this "wise-guy" approach to the market can prevent you from realizing perhaps the most important benefit of stock splits—long-term growth. In our study, one month after the effective date of their splits, 58 percent of the companies were enjoying split-adjusted share prices that exceeded the peak price during the announcement-effective date gap. So the best ways to profit from splits may be to preserve your holdings in issues that split and acquire them if you don't yet have them.

But don't expect consistent performance. Many variables, such as market conditions and the strength of the companies involved, can affect share price as much as split factors. Our firm belief is that you should manage your stock portfolio for growth over an extended period and not have your vision clouded by quick-buck mirages. Market-timers are courting disaster.

If you feel compelled to dabble in this area, here are several guidelines suggested by our research: If you're considering purchase of a stock and learn that it will split, you might want to defer your acquisition until just after the split effective date. In our sample, 89 percent of the stocks traded at a lower split-adjusted price on the effective date than the inflated price bid up during the announcement-effective date gap.

And if you're looking to exit a stock, doing it just before the effective date may be preferable to waiting; as noted, share prices typically fall from their interim highs.

Scoring:

Score 4 points for a), 3 for c), 2 for d), 0 for b).

Question 6—

The Bond Market provides a place for the sale and purchase of bonds. Which of the following statements about bonds is false?

a) Bonds are safer investments than stocks because your principal is guaranteed, even if you sell bonds in the secondary market prior to maturity.

b) Changes in interest rates will affect the price of bonds.

c) If you buy bonds through your broker, you'll pay a commission.

d) "Laddering" a portfolio of bonds is a strategy to even out fluctuations in interest rates.

Let's look at some basics about bonds before addressing Question 6. A bond is essentially an IOU given to you by the federal or state government, a municipality, or a corporation, to name the most popular types. The issuer promises to pay you interest (coupon rate) for a specified period of time (maturity) and then return your principal to you. Federal and state government agencies use the proceeds of bond offerings to finance a broad range of activities. Municipalities issue bonds to underwrite such projects as highway improvement, school modernization, and other civic initiatives. Corporations issue them to pay for expansion and improvements.

Bonds are popular investments, as they promise some return with apparently minimal peril to your principal. Yet there are risks involved. Bonds are only as secure as the organizations that issue them are stable. Invest in a bond and you become a creditor of the issuing organization. You're lending them money that you hope they'll pay back, along with interest. But the issuing organization could falter or fail, taking your investment down the tubes with them.

Bonds always are backed by "the full faith and credit" of the issuing municipality, corporation, or agency. Just what does this pledge mean to us as investors? We can get some guidance from independent rating services, such as Moody's Investors Service and Standard & Poor's, which evaluate and rate the financial strength of issuers and their bonds. For example, S&P ratings are:

- ▣ AAA—Extremely strong capacity to meet its financial commitments.

- ▣ AA—Very strong.

- ▣ A—Strong.

- ▣ BBB—Adequate.

- ▣ BB—Can meet obligations currently but faces major ongoing uncertainties that could lead to inadequate financial capacity.

- ▣ B—More vulnerable than BB but still capable currently.

- ▣ CCC—Currently vulnerable in its ability to meet its financial commitments.

- ▣ CC—Currently highly vulnerable.

In S&P rankings, bonds rated less than BBB are considered "below investment grade" and highly speculative as a result.

In some cases, issuers acquire insurance coverage for their bonds to provide additional safety for purchasers; investors pay a price for this protection in the form of lower interest rates. The general rule is: The safer the bond, the lower the interest rate; the riskier the bond, the greater the possible return. It's important to remember this rule when you encounter advertisements "guaranteeing" a high interest rate. One might ask, "Guaranteed by whom?" If the ads don't mention that—and few of them will—you're best advised to walk away.

Another key point to remember about bonds is that, while each has a face value, the actual value varies at any time, based on prevailing interest rates. There's an inverse relationship between bond value and interest rates. Imagine that you purchase a corporate bond with a 10-year maturity and an interest rate of 5 percent. What happens if interest rates rise to 6 percent the following year? You're locked into your 5 percent, but new investors can choose bonds paying 6 percent. They wouldn't want to buy yours because of the better deals available. To sell your bond, you would have to reduce its price to make it competitive with newly issued 6 percent bonds. On the other hand, should interest rates drop to 4 percent when your bond is bringing 5 percent, your bond becomes more valuable at sale, even though its face value hasn't changed.

Because of the impact of inflation, perhaps the best measure of any bond's current value is its *yield to maturity*, which equals interest received from the time you purchase the bond until it matures, plus any gain or loss generated from the difference between your purchase price and maturity value.

With this information in hand, let's take a closer look at Question 6:

Answer a) is false and the best response to this question. Bonds are not always safer than stocks. Neither the return on principal nor the principal itself is necessarily guaranteed, injecting an element of risk into the bond business.

As noted, interest rates always affect bond values, so answer b) is true.

On answer c), brokers are paid through a charge akin to commission called a *mark-up*. They buy bonds at what might be thought of as the wholesale value, mark them up, then sell them to us at the retail value, making their money off the difference. There's nothing shady about this; virtually every merchant does the same thing, whether their products are bonds or babushkas. However, it does make it imperative for us to understand what the market is currently yielding and the yield to maturity on our bonds. That way, we'll know if our brokers' mark-ups are competitive and reasonable.

As for answer d), *laddering* a portfolio of bonds is indeed a strategy to even out the changes produced by fluctuating interest rates, and thereby reduce risk. The centerpiece of laddering is the purchase of bonds with various maturities. In this scenario, if you have $50,000 to invest, you might consider purchasing five $10,000 bonds with different maturities. One might have a two-year maturity, the second a three-year maturity, another a five-year maturity, the fourth a seven-year maturity, and the final bond will offer a 10-year maturity. Over the course of the next 10 years, interest rates likely will fluctuate. But with the staggered maturity schedule of your bonds, you'll likely catch both the interest peaks and valleys, evening out the differences and giving you (pretty much) the return you projected.

Laddering is a useful long-term approach, and you can "front-end" or "back-end" your ladder to reflect current economic conditions. For example, if interest rates are at historically low levels when you purchase your bonds, and the possibility of rising interest rates is strong, you may want to "front-end" your portfolio by purchasing shorter maturities; as your bonds mature, they'll create cash that will allow you to acquire new bonds with higher interest rates. If prevailing interest rates are unusually high, do the reverse—"back-end" your portfolio so that more of your bonds are locked in at higher interest rates.

Scoring:

Score 4 points for a), 0 for any other answer.

	Scoring for Chapter 3	
	Highest Possible Score	**Your Score**
Question 1	1	_____
Question 2	1	_____
Question 3	4	_____
Question 4	4	_____
Question 5	4	_____
Question 6	4	_____
CHAPTER TOTALS	18	_____

4 The Role of Economics, or Who the Heck is Alan Greenspan?

We tend to evaluate stocks on their perceived individual merits: This company offers a strong management team; that one has products with international appeal; a third has been trading well below its value. But if we base our acquisition, hold, and sell decisions on these individual characteristics alone, we may lose sight of the macro forces at play in the stock market—and other investment forums.

Stocks don't operate in a vacuum. They play in a global market that can be shaped or buffeted by such powerful forces as inflation, disease, famine, natural calamities, war, and other departures from the quotidian. A dramatic illustration of the power of macro forces occurred in the late 1990s when the stock market was battered by the so-called "Asian flu" (the unexpected collapse of the economy in several countries in Asia). Companies in which you own stock may have had little direct contact with the affected nations, yet their stock prices plummeted nevertheless. That was just one painful example of how global interrelatedness—a macro force—can influence all investments.

We can't really anticipate wars or natural disasters, although we can understand that they *will* happen and that they *will* affect us. We *can* explore and grasp the discipline of economics. Economics has been dismissed as "the dreary science," yet economic forces always have an impact on our investments, whether or not we understand those forces.

It's more difficult than ever to focus on the big picture, overwhelmed as we are by 'round-the-clock financial networks and analysts' recommendations that often emphasize individual securities rather than macro forces. As a result, we tend to rely on past performance as our main indicator for investment decisions. While past performance is a useful measure of comparison to investments of the same type, it tells us little about the performance of any sector relative to the economy or business cycles. In short, past performance ignores macro forces. If we rely on it exclusively, we may make the classic mistake of chasing performance in an environment where 3-year or 5-year track records mean very little.

Investment sectors and philosophies come in and out of favor due, in part, to economic conditions. Even a rudimentary understanding of economics will help tame our fear and greed and lead us to rational, long-term investing choices.

Which brings us to Alan Greenspan. In investment circles, perhaps no name is uttered with as much respect, fear, and loathing. Greenspan is chairman of the Federal Reserve Board, the institution with an outsized effect on monetary policy for the United States—and by extension, for much of the world. The Federal Reserve helps shape macroeconomic forces by controlling the supply of money and by setting the discount interest rates that eventually ripple through the entire economy.

Greenspan was appointed to the Fed post by President Reagan in 1987, so he's served in his position longer than any president served in his. Greenspan's every move and utterance are parsed by analysts as relentlessly and ridiculously as Kremlinologists used to analyze Politburo pronouncements. When

Greenspan chastised investors a few years ago for "irrational exuberance," he single-handedly took some of the wind from the sails of the tech boom. "Irrational exuberance," meanwhile, entered the language, a neologism mouthed by analysts and amateurs alike.

Our questions in this chapter are aimed at enhancing your understanding of macroeconomic forces. These are to be understood and accounted for but never worshipped. In 1994, when *U.S. News & World Report* asked Warren Buffett, CEO of Berkshire Hathaway Inc. and one of the most successful stock market investors of all time, about the inordinate influence of Greenspan, he had this to say:

"If...Greenspan were to whisper to me what his monetary policy was going to be over the next two years, it wouldn't change one thing I do."

So much for the Grand Pooh-bah of macroeconomics.

Question 1—

Which of these statements about inflation is true?

a) Inflation always is a negative economic indicator.

b) All segments of society suffer during inflation.

c) Inflation can be prevented by appropriate government intervention.

d) As a rule, inflation means a decrease in your purchasing power.

At its simplest, inflation may be defined as the increase in prices over a set period of time, often produced when demand exceeds supply. Typically, inflation is measured on an annual basis. Over the past 25 years in the United States, the average annual inflation rate has been 4.8 percent. In other words, the basket of goods and services you purchased 25 years ago would cost you 223 percent more today. That's a pretty clear decrease in your purchasing power, so d) is the best answer.

While inflation hurts, it's not always a signal that the economy is faring poorly. Modest inflation can be an indication that the economy is expanding, with output trying to catch up with demand. But the phenomenon is most harmful when inflation is combined with a struggling economy. Prices may be rising, but our ability to pay for goods doesn't keep pace.

Not all segments of society are affected equally by inflation. Because prices are higher, some companies will experience increased profits, even if forced to pay higher wages and benefits. On the down side, those living on fixed incomes feel the effects of inflation most acutely. They have no opportunity to increase their income as so many workers do during inflationary periods, so their fixed income buys them less than it used to.

It's also important to remember that inflation is an average that doesn't necessarily relate to any one sector. Consider higher education. One of the reasons that saving for college education is so challenging these days is that the rate of inflation of college tuition has been running at about 6 percent annually, far outstripping the average inflation rate for the economy. If you're a student or parent struggling to save for college, you're well aware that inflation has a disproportionate impact on you.

Finally, while it may be comforting to think that government action can prevent inflation, history has shown that official monetary policies often have an ameliorating effect rather than a preventive one. When macroeconomic forces are at work, even the most well-intended and powerful government may be a minor player. However, if you understand inflation and government attempts to control it, you'll also appreciate the impact on the market. You'll be well-positioned to make sound buy-sell decisions rather than those based on—Dare we say it?—irrational exuberance or despair.

Scoring:

Score 4 points for d). Since government intervention can help control, if not prevent, inflation, give yourself 2 points for c). Score 0 for a) and b).

Question 2—

If you present a dollar bill at your local U.S. Treasury Office and demand its equivalent in gold, you:

a) Will be given a small bag of gold dust.

b) Will be permitted to choose between a tiny gold ingot and a piece of gold jewelry.

c) Will be advised that the U.S. no longer uses a gold standard.

d) Will be asked to walk a straight line.

For many years, much of the world used what might be thought of as a "classic" gold standard. Britain is credited with being the first country to adopt the gold standard in 1816; the United States came on board in 1873. The premise was that any government on the gold standard was obliged to exchange paper money for a fixed amount of gold, and to maintain appropriate gold reserves to honor any and all exchanges.

Since the supply of gold was relatively constant, prices could vary through a narrow range only, and inflation was held in check. Indeed, while the gold standard prevailed, inflation was a relatively insignificant phenomenon throughout the world. But this stability also had its price as governments, entrusting a hands-off mechanism to regulate monetary policy, had little opportunity to intervene.

The gold standard began to totter in the wake of the hardships occasioned by World War I, when a number of European nations adopted a modified version known as the *gold exchange standard*, where currencies were pegged primarily to the British pound or American dollar and not to gold itself. More money was printed and circulated through the system, enabling countries to pay their debts but triggering a grave inflationary spiral.

In fact, some economists attribute the Great Depression to the abandonment of the classic gold standard, although as most complex international events, this one likely was the result of multiple causes. Even today, some economists blame the paper money standard for inflation, arguing that systems that rely on government intervention rather than automatic, gold-backed controls are subject to mistakes that can trigger or strengthen inflation. It seems unlikely that the nations of the world will return to the gold standard anytime soon.

The United States began its retreat from the classic gold standard as early as 1913, when it created the Federal Reserve System (Fed). The gold standard remained, but this new institution was poised to exert control over U.S. monetary policy—powers it ultimately would implement—rather than relying on the creaks and groans of the mechanical gold standard.

In 1933, the U.S. went off the classic gold standard and adopted a *modified gold bullion standard*. It abandoned the gold standard for good in 1971. Our gold remains tucked safely and soundly into Fort Knox, but without a gold standard, it's more a commodity than a guarantee of paper money or a tool to regulate inflation. Today, it's the Fed that controls monetary policy, expanding or contracting the money supply without worrying about a gold guarantee.

Scoring:

With the demise of the gold standard, the best answer to this question, worth 4 points, is c). Give yourself 1 point for d). We don't think security at the Treasury office will treat you as if you were under the influence of alcohol, but you never know.

Question 3—

The nation's money supply is known to economists by this shorthand designation:

a) Cash cache.

b) M1.

c) M2.

d) ATM (for All The Marbles).

The money supply may not seem terribly important to us as individual investors, but it can be an important measure for the Federal Reserve as a guide for its monetary control policies. The Fed typically calculates the money supply in two measures. M1 might be thought of us all the money in circulation, including cash and coins, plus checking account balances at banks.

M2 is a broader measure; in addition to everything counted in M1, it includes a number of savings vehicles, such as savings accounts, certificates of deposit, and money market accounts. M1 tells us the amount of cash available now. M2 suggests the amount of money currently available, plus the volume that could easily be converted to cash. Both measures are in trillions of dollars, but M2 usually runs about 3 1/2 times the size of M1.

The Fed tracks the Ms (M1 and M2) to identify swings in liquidity that could lead it to consider interest rate modifications or other intervention, such as changing the reserve requirement for banks and buying or selling government bonds (called open-market operations). All such actions manipulate the money supply in the hope of controlling inflation, output, unemployment, and spending.

Both money supply measures sound very much like a James Bond script (*007? M1 here.*) but knowing what they are will help you understand some of the macro economic forces at play in investing.

Scoring:

Score 2 points for either b) or c), as both are correct. Score 0 points for other answers.

Question 4—

The Federal Reserve System adjusts interest rates to:

a) Maintain growth in the economy while controlling inflation.

b) Assist investors in the stock and bond markets.

c) Make it easier for banks to lend money and for businesses to get credit.

d) Encourage consumer spending.

Created in 1913 by an act of Congress, the "Fed," as it's popularly known, is the central banking system of the United States. Controlled by a seven-member board of governors and a chairman, the Fed has headquarters in Washington, DC, and 12 district banks across the nation. Banks that are members of the Fed hold stock in those regional facilities, although they typically have little say in policy. That's left to the board of governors, and a powerful panel it is. Governors have 14-year terms; perhaps only federal judges have longer stints in office. While the chairman and governors are appointed by the president and confirmed by the Senate, their policy decisions are not subject to congressional or executive approval or modification. Nor does the chairman leave office when the president does. What the Fed says, goes.

The Fed has broad authority to oversee banks in all their financial services. But it's perhaps best known for two of its regulatory roles: controlling the supply of money and setting the discount borrowing rate, that is, the rate at which the Fed lends money to banks.

If the Fed believes that the nation's money supply is growing too slowly to meet the nation's needs, it can purchase U.S. Treasury securities on the open market, injecting a huge cash flow into the system and making the entire economy more liquid. Conversely, if the money supply appears to be growing so fast that inflation is a threat, the Fed may sell Treasury securities, taking cash from the system and reducing bank reserves.

Its impact on credit interest rates is just as profound. At certain points in the business cycle, the demand for goods and services may exceed supply, allowing companies to raise prices. Why would they do that? Because the market will bear it. If demand is great, customers will be forced to absorb the price increases. (We see this price spiral now in higher education. Colleges and universities implement increase after increase in their tuition, yet enrollment keeps increasing. Apparently, students and parents will pay the price, no matter what it is, for the educational institutions of their choice. If this can happen with entities that are ostensibly not-for-profit, imagine what for-profit companies will do.) Left unattended, rounds of price hikes could set off rampant inflation.

However, if the Fed sees that the economy is overheating—growing at a rate so fast that inflation could be triggered—it can raise the interest rate it charges to banks. This flows throughout the economy, ultimately increasing the interest rate to businesses looking to borrow money and even to us as consumers. We see it in the form of higher interest rates on loans we seek for home improvements or new car purchases. Borrowing is discouraged, and the economy cools.

The reverse is also true. When the economy seems too sluggish, the Fed may lower its discount rate. This action, as well, will be felt throughout the economy, encouraging companies and consumers to borrow money and get the economy percolating.

This is a delicate balancing act that the Fed typically performs at regularly scheduled meetings, although it's free to intervene whenever it chooses. During the slump of 2001, for example, the Fed lowered its discount rate 11 times—sometimes at scheduled meetings, sometimes on an ad hoc basis—to pump some life into the economy. These actions were widely anticipated, welcomed, or feared, depending on the viewpoint of the observer, because of their potential impact on the markets.

Interest rates *will* affect market performances—that's why they're so anxiously anticipated and hotly debated. The Fed's discount rate is one of those macro forces that will play an important role in your holdings. It can send the market up or down, depending on whether investors regard any fix by the Fed as the right treatment for an economic malaise. The stocks you hold can be carried along in the upward or downward trend, irrespective of the fundamental values of the companies in your portfolio.

Understanding the impact of the Fed as a macro force will keep you from ill-considered actions in a Fed-inspired market swing. You'll make your buy-sell decisions rationally, based on the strength of the stocks you're considering, and not be unduly influenced by the trend *du jour,* which can be difficult to interpret. For example, if the Fed increases interest rates, the market may drop in anticipation of a cooling economy. Yet if the Fed is expected to hike interest rates and doesn't, that too could send the market tumbling as an indication that the economy isn't as strong as we thought. Trying to predict market responses to Fed actions is frustrating and unproductive. Instead, don't worry unduly about the short-term impact on your investments.

Scoring:

Answer a) is best, since maintaining the balance between growth and inflation always is the Fed's primary goal. Score 4 points for a). However, since specific Fed actions may benefit large sectors, such as investors, businesses, or consumers, score 2 points for any answer other than a).

Question 5—

Which of the following is not considered a "leading indicator"?

a) M2.

b) Initial unemployment claims.

c) Unemployment rate.

d) Plant and equipment orders.

This question deals with indicators, certain economic measures that experts maintain can give us a macro view of our economy and perhaps serve as a guide to individual investors. Indicators come in three flavors—leading indicators, which indicate where we're headed; lagging indicators, which tell us where we've been; and coincident indicators, which let us know where we are now.

Leading indicators include:

- ◙ Average work week (manufacturing).

- ◙ Initial unemployment claims.

- ◙ Manufacturers' new orders for products (consumer goods).

- ◙ Vendor performance.

- ◙ Plant and equipment orders.

- ◙ New private housing units authorized by local building permits.

- ◙ Change in manufacturers' unfilled orders (durable goods).

- ◙ Change in sensitive materials prices.

- ◙ Stock prices (S&P 500).

- ◙ M2.

- ◙ Index of consumer expectations.

The common feature of leading indicators is that they're all thought to have some predictive value. The Conference Board, a private, nonprofit entity, aggregates all the leading indicators in the LEI (Leading Economic Indicators), which helps reduce the sum of these measures to a single, understandable number.

Lagging indicators are:

- ◙ Unemployment rate.

- ◙ Business spending.

- ◙ Unit labor costs.

- ▣ Bank loans outstanding.

- ▣ Bank interest rates.

- ▣ Book value of manufacturing and trade inventories.

As with leading indicators, lagging indicators often are aggregated in a single index. The third category, coincident indicators, includes:

- ▣ Non-farm payroll workers.

- ▣ Personal income less transfer payments.

- ▣ Industrial production.

- ▣ Manufacturing.

- ▣ Trade sales.

Economists go to great lengths to study all indicators to help them understand where our economy is in what's known as a "business cycle," a sustained upward or downward trend. The National Bureau of Economic Research (NBER) is the designated statistician of business cycles; it's NBER that formally indicates when we're in an expansion or a recession, for example, although most of us come to that realization well in advance of any official pronouncement.

Business cycles typically are long, at least by our standards as individual investors. According to NBER, the 41 recessions the United States experienced between 1802 and 1997 averaged nearly 18 months in length; expansions during that period lasted for an average of almost 38 months. Because these periods tend to take root, there could well be some benefit from government intervention, either to extend an expansion or prevent or end a recession. That's why economists pore over all categories of indicators so intently—to see what actions might best prolong or reverse the current business cycle.

The problem is that indicators often don't indicate very much, at least where overall market performance is concerned. The indicators looked favorable, to cite one example, in the summer of 1987...just before the stock market took its most precipitous drop since the Great Depression. If you followed the sunny summer forecast of the indicators, you took a hard fall come October.

Often what we get with indicators might be thought of as the Toilet Paper Effect. When a community feels threatened, residents rush to the supermarket to stock up on the basic goods they think they'll need to get them through the coming emergency. You, of course, act more rationally and eschew this frantic hoarding, and you feel pretty smug when the scare turns out to be a false alarm. But when you get to the store, it's out of toilet paper just the same.

Indicators can create much the same stampeding. They may or may not be a good guideline for investing, but they often are excellent at forecasting how investors as a group will act. If you understand the herd mentality that can function as a macro economic force, you'll have a deeper appreciation for market swings; those swings won't rush you to an ill-considered or premature buy-sell decision.

Scoring:

Among the indicators listed, only c) is a lagging indicator rather than a leading indicator. Score 4 points for c), 0 for any other answer.

	Scoring for Chapter 4	
	Highest Possible Score	**Your Score**
Question 1	4	_____
Question 2	4	_____
Question 3	2	_____
Question 4	4	_____
Question 5	4	_____
CHAPTER TOTALS	18	_____

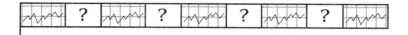

5 The International Game— Is It Time for You to Go Global?

E ver since George Washington cautioned his young country to stay out of entangling alliances, Americans have felt ambivalent about international affairs. We actively pursue international trade, but we're not averse to throwing up a protective tariff to keep out foreign-made goods. We avoid distant conflicts only to step into them when we perceive a threat to our national interest, however malleable the definition of that interest might be. We support the United Nations, but whose name is that up there on the delinquent dues list?

This ambivalence about global affairs often carries over to the decisions of individual investors. Many consider themselves quite cosmopolitan but avoid stocks of companies based outside the United States.

This approach is not without some logic. When we invest in foreign companies, we're taking a flyer on businesses about which we may not receive regular reports. It can be hard to keep up with their progress—they don't necessarily make the day's headlines on CNN—and this apparent information vacuum can give pause to any investor.

The wide reach of the Internet has helped to fill the information gap. Today, following the fortunes of any foreign-based company—or international mutual fund—can be as simple as going online. The Internet has wrought even more profound changes in global commerce. Companies in search of raw materials can stage online auctions and find dozens of potential suppliers—some of them domestic, some of them not—eager to bid. The Internet has affected the other end of the production line as well. Manufacturers can identify buyers for their products across the globe by hopping on the Web.

Thus, the inevitable appeal of electronic commerce has helped to produce a global economy—although we may not have been fully aware that it was happening. The investment landscape has seen corresponding changes. Even if you're determined to "buy American" exclusively, that's becoming increasingly difficult. You may want to invest in a domestic automaker, to cite one example, only to find that the vehicles are assembled outside the United States Cross-border partnerships are common in other industries as well.

How popular are the stocks of foreign companies? According to the U.S. Securities and Exchange Commission, foreign stocks represented almost 10 percent of all securities held by Americans at the end of 1997. The number of foreign companies registered with the SEC grew from 134 in 1990 to more than 1,100 by 1998.

As Jeremy Siegel notes in his book, *Stocks for the Long Run,* U.S. stocks comprised almost 90 percent of the world's equity capitalization at the end of World War II. Today, they constitute less than half of the world's stock values. "...for many years, foreign markets were almost exclusively the domain of native investors, considered too remote and risky to be entertained by outsiders. But no longer. Globalization is the financial buzzword of the decade," Siegel says. "The United States, once the unchallenged giant of capital markets, has become only one of many countries in which investors can accumulate wealth."

In short, global markets can mean opportunity. The stock of foreign companies, or a mutual fund of such stocks, can be a key element in the diversification of your portfolio. That, in turn, can reduce overall portfolio risk and improve your return. The more familiar you become with international markets, the fewer reservations you'll have about investing in those markets.

Our questions in this chapter are designed to introduce you to some important aspects of international markets. This will be a cursory introduction, but it could whet your appetite for more. And if you're still leery about international markets after you finish this chapter—*Vive la differance!*

Question 1—

Which of these entities is not an important proponent for, and force in, international commerce and development?

a) World Trade Organization.

b) International Monetary Fund.

c) Bank for International Settlements.

d) International Forum on Globalization.

This question focuses the spotlight on several of the most prominent and powerful players in international economics and development. Though it may be lower profile than others, the Bank for International Settlements may be the granddaddy of international economics institutions. It was created in 1930 as a vehicle to supervise the reparations imposed on Germany after World War I.

Since then, the bank has expanded and taken on a number of key functions. From its headquarters in Basel, Switzerland, it provides a forum for central bank cooperation, hoping that its efforts will foster financial stability throughout the world. It conducts and disseminates research aimed at monetary and financial stability and offers recommendations to the financial community based on that research.

The bank also performs more traditional functions, such as reserve management and gold transactions for its customers. In March 2000, its holdings in currency deposits totaled $128 billion, representing about 7 percent of the world's foreign exchange reserves. This bank may be low-profile, but $128 billion ain't chump change.

The International Monetary Fund (IMF) may be the best known of these organizations. It emerged from a 1944 United Nations conference in Bretton Woods, New Hampshire, with 45 nations participating. Today, IMF includes 183 member countries and an enormous staff or more than 2,600 at its Washington, DC, headquarters.

IMF promotes international monetary cooperation, exchange stability, and orderly exchange arrangements. It fosters economic growth that it hopes will lead to robust employment, and it provides temporary financial assistance to countries to help ease their international trade debts.

It is for this latter function that IMF may be best known. To its borrowers, it issues what are called "Special Drawing Rights," an innocuous-sounding accounting unit whose name belies its punch. In February 2002, outstanding SDRs to 88 nations totaled about $77 billion.

The World Trade Organization (WTO) is a relatively young organization formed in 1995, although it was based on a number of predecessor entities. Headquartered in Geneva and boasting 144 member countries, WTO bills itself as the only global organization dealing with the rules of trade among nations. It oversees bilateral and multilateral agreements that cover such things as open markets, tariffs, export/import protocols, and other aspects of international trade.

"The result," WTO says, "is assurance. Consumers and producers know that they can enjoy secure supplies and greater choice of the finished products, components, raw materials and services that they use. Producers and exporters know that foreign markets will remain open to them. The result is also a more prosperous, peaceful and accountable economic world."

Prosperity, peace, accountability—who could argue with that? Yet people do, as these powerful organizations routinely generate controversy that seems to reflect the ongoing ambivalence of many about globalization. When China sought WTO membership, for example, it sparked a worldwide debate about whether that country's human rights policies made it a fit candidate for admission. In the United States, the debate became part of a protracted lobbying campaign that saw both sides pour in millions of dollars. Congress finally approved China's membership, and she entered the WTO on December 11, 2001.

That may have been a one-shot issue, but the controversy over WTO's role in globalization—and the impact of globalization itself—continues to burn. WTO meetings, such as a session in Seattle—routinely inspire protests that occasionally turn violent, prompting host cities to undertake extraordinary security measures.

Among the groups leading the opposition is the International Forum on Globalization (IFG), which conducted a Seattle "teach-in" that paralleled the WTO meeting. IFG is responding to what it considers "the effective takeover of global governance by transnational corporations and the international trade bureaucracies that they established."

In a nutshell, IFG argues that globalization, as now practiced, promotes development at the expense of the environment; diminishes the ability of local communities, states, and even nations to control their own destinies; triggers sharp increases in unemployment due to automation; and reinforces the "economic colonization of southern countries by northern countries." WTO has been a principal target of IFG's wrath, but it also skewers IMF, the World Bank, and other international institutions and treaties.

While its mechanics and outcomes likely will be debated for some time to come, globalization is here to stay. This is one genie that won't fit back in the bottle.

Scoring:

> The key word in the question is "proponent." IFG could be considered a force in globalization; it's anything but a proponent. Score 4 points for d), 0 for any other answer.

Question 2—

The best definition for "bourse" is:

a) The stock exchange of Paris.

b) Investors who behave in an unmannerly fashion.

c) Any venue where securities or commodities are bought and sold regularly.

d) People who go on and on about themselves.

While Americans may be most familiar with the principal stock exchanges of their own nation, countries around the world—many large cities as well—host stock exchanges. A common generic term for such exchanges is *bourse*. So when you hear people refer to the bourse, they may be discussing the local stock exchange.

However, they also may be talking about the stock exchange of Paris, which is known as the Bourse. A number of other cities call their stock exchanges bourse as well, so it's important to know whether the discussion involves the bourse, a general term, or the Bourse, a specific title.

Scoring:

> Both a) and c) are equally correct; score 2 points for either answer. We've met a few boors and a few other bores in our day, but the financial industry has no special name for them.

Question 3—

Among these stock exchanges, which is the oldest?

a) SWX Swiss Exchange.

b) National Stock Exchange of India.

c) London Stock Exchange.

d) Tel Aviv Stock Exchange.

There are dozens of stock exchanges throughout the world, presenting a compelling variety of purposes and styles. Most commonly, though, they were developed to provide local companies with a vehicle for raising capital, and an opportunity for investors to deliver that capital—with a profit anticipated, of course.

Some have a financial education mission as well. The Australian Stock Exchange (ASX), for example, staged a Web-based game in 2002 that tested players' investment skills. Each was given a hypothetical $50,000 to invest over an eight-week period. The contest, no doubt, generated a lot of buzz about, and interest in, ASX.

Few exchanges have as lengthy or as colorful a history as the London Stock Exchange. It was formed in 1760 by a group of 150 brokers who were kicked out of the Royal Exchange for rowdiness. The formative discussions took place, improbably, at an establishment called Jonathan's Coffee House.

The London Exchange actually dates its founding to 1801, when it formally came under regulation for the first time, but it's still older by far than any of the other exchanges listed here. Just before its 200th birthday, the exchange came full circle when it became a publicly held company—a far cry from its clubby beginnings.

Switzerland is an important financial center; as such, you would expect it to have an important stock exchange. It does, but the Swiss Exchange is of recent vintage. In fact, until 1995, independent stock exchanges flourished in three Swiss cities— Geneva (founded in 1850), Zurich (1873), and Basel (1876). These three historic exchanges united to form SWX.

The stock exchanges in India and Tel Aviv are relatively young as well. While India has other stock exchanges, the National Stock Exchange of India was created in 1992 as a tax-paying entity. In Israel, informal stock trading dates to 1935. The Tel Aviv Stock Exchange, however, didn't begin formal operations until 1953, five years after the founding of Israel as a nation.

Any of the world's stock exchanges may deal in securities that could prove to be attractive investments for you. Far from being exotic, many goods produced by companies based outside the United States are popular with American consumers. Enjoy a Dunkin' Donut and you're biting into a little piece of Great Britain. Feed your toddlers Gerber baby food and you've patronized a Swiss business. Store that food in a Frigidaire appliance and you're cooling it with a Swedish product. Talk to friends on your nifty Nokia cellular phone and you have a Finnish firm to thank for the convenience. All are top companies; they, and many other firms outside the United States, can be considered investment targets.

If you're still concerned about the stability and reliability of stock exchanges abroad, be aware that most are regulated and belong to such trade organizations as the World Federation of Stock Exchanges and the International Options Market Association. The World Federation boasts 56 members that, according to the organization, account for more than 97 percent of world stock market capitalization, meaning that just about everybody who's anybody is a member. The federation imposes certain requirements on is members and performs due diligence on membership candidates—all of which should serve to inspire confidence in stock exchanges outside the United States.

Scoring:
If you answered c), give yourself 4 points.

Question 4—
Which of these is *not* a defining characteristic of emerging nations?

a) High unemployment.

b) Low or moderate per capita income.

c) Undeveloped capital markets.

d) Undeveloped industrial sectors.

There are many ways to categorize the nations of the world. One useful framework for investors is to think of countries as developing, underdeveloped, or emerging. In his book, *The Investor's Guide to Emerging Markets,* veteran mutual fund manager Mark Mobius notes the most widely held definition: "Emerging nations are those with low or moderate per capita income, undeveloped capital markets, and weak or nonexistent industry." Thus, the correct answer to Question 4 is a), since unemployment rates play no role in this categorization.

(For the record, Mobius also credits several alternative definitions of emerging nations. In another version, an emerging nation is "one whose market represents less than 3 percent of the world's stock market capitalization.")

Emerging nations are plentiful, numbering more than 120 according to the classic definition. Not all are potential targets for your investment; some lack stock markets, and still others forbid or restrict foreign investment. Even when these countries are stricken from the list, the total is healthy and inviting. Should you consider investing in these markets?

For many, the answer is a resounding yes. Recent years have brought the creation of many mutual funds that target emerging economies. Mobius serves as president of several such entities, including the Templeton Emerging Markets Fund. The attraction to these markets is the vast untapped potential of their economies. The shift from agrarian to industrial emphasis can mean huge gains for the companies changing the paradigm—and for those who invest in such companies.

But where foreign investments are concerned, many of us tend to see more risk than opportunity. Mobius identifies eight types of risk associated with emerging markets:

- Political risks.
- Currency risks.
- Company risks.
- Investment risks.
- Broker risks.
- Settlement risks.
- Safekeeping risks.
- Operational risks.

Risk, in all its incarnations, must be acknowledged, but are the risks different or their potential impact less with domestic investment? Consider operational risk, which Mobius defines as "...[R]isks arising from inadequate procedures or audit standards." The public disgrace and fall of Enron, Arthur Andersen, WorldCom, and other high-profile American companies demonstrated pretty conclusively that operational risk is not the exclusive preserve of emerging nations.

Or how about political risk, the threat that political developments will create an unstable environment? To be sure, we find those in emerging countries, but the tragic events of 9/11 demonstrated that even well-developed nations aren't immune from destabilizing events.

Looked at most charitably, our reluctance to invest in emerging economies may be a product of inadequate information about those markets. Viewed less kindly, what may be operating here is bias, pure and simple.

Research will help us overcome any prejudices and identify the most promising opportunities in emerging nations. Keep an open mind on this type of investment. It could add an element to your portfolio that can't be matched elsewhere. Study the potential and the dangers, just as you would for any other investment, and you'll come to a rational decision free of bias or misinformation.

Scoring:

Score 4 points for a), 0 for all other answers.

Question 5—

Which of these is a means of investing in companies based outside the United States?

a) Buying shares directly in foreign markets.

    b) Purchasing mutual funds that invest internationally.

    c) Acquiring American Depositary Receipts.

    d) All of the above.

The international business landscape is colorful and inviting if you know how to structure your investments. You have a number of options.

One option is to invest directly in foreign companies in the markets in which they trade. At times, this can be more difficult than it seems. A number of stock exchanges around the world are not open to foreigners, or those governments may limit foreign investment in indigenous companies. Getting timely information about your target investments can be troublesome as well; reporting requirements differ from country to country. The Internet will be a valuable information source for you, yet it must be acknowledged that online reports may not have precisely the data you need, or may not be available in a timely fashion.

Direct foreign investment poses other challenges. For instance, if your target company pays dividends, will you receive them in U.S. dollars or the local currency? If you receive them in the local currency, you'll incur exchange fees that must be factored into your overall return projections for each stock. Frequent exchanges can be an inconvenience as well.

Clearly, investing directly in a foreign market requires thorough knowledge of local investment regulations, and an equally comprehensive understanding of the policies and practices of the companies involved. Reliable, timely information is the key. If you're not convinced that you could acquire all the data necessary, you might want to consider other options.

Another route is investing in mutual funds that target foreign markets. The number of such funds has grown spectacularly.

There are now about 2,100 mutual funds that specialize in foreign markets; many of them maintain offices—and an important presence—in those markets. In fact, the field is so crowded that these specialists have developed subspecialties. You can find funds that target developed nations or emerging markets; those that deal in a single continent; funds that focus on one market sector, technology, say, across the entire world. This sounds very much like the scope of domestic mutual funds; indeed, the international field is quite similar in this respect. Morningstar, one of the most popular mutual fund ratings services, lists these specialties of international funds:

- ▣ Foreign Stock.
- ▣ World Stock (or Global, which includes the United States).
- ▣ International Hybrid.
- ▣ Europe.
- ▣ Japan.
- ▣ Latin America.
- ▣ Diversified Pacific Asia.
- ▣ Pacific/Asia excluding Japan.
- ▣ Diversified Emerging Markets.
- ▣ International Bond.
- ▣ Emerging Markets Bond.

Mutual funds that target foreign markets offer two important possibilities: greater return and portfolio diversification. We've gone beyond the concept stage on this, as a number of credible studies have confirmed that adding an overseas component to your investments can help reduce overall portfolio fluctuation and enhance return. Foreign markets sometimes respond to different forces than the U.S. market does, and so their performance may vary accordingly.

Consider a performance comparison of the MSCI EAFE Index, a popular measure of stocks in well-developed foreign markets, and the S&P 500, a leading index of American stocks. In 1988, when the S&P registered a solid gain of 16.61 percent, the MSCI EAFE index soared 28.59 percent. But in 1995, when the S&P recorded a decade-best gain of 37.58 percent, the MSCI EAFE was up a more modest 11.55 percent. For investors, stocks traded on each of these exchanges can be complementary, smoothing out performance aberrations.

Mutual funds also can help you overcome the information gap. They've done the bulk of the research for you. They'll provide that data, as well as timely reports, as a matter of course. Your principal research job becomes checking out the fund manager to make sure of an investing philosophy that's compatible with yours.

A third option for investing in foreign companies is to target businesses based outside the U.S. that trade in American markets. For most such companies, stocks are traded as American Depositary Receipts (ADRs) that are issued by U.S. depositary banks. If you own an ADR, you have the right to demand the actual shares that it represents, but most investors find it more convenient to maintain the ADR. The price of an ADR corresponds to the share price in the foreign market, but that price is adjusted to the ratio of ADRs to shares in the headquarters' country.

There are costs associated with ADRs. Depositary banks charge fees for their services, and you must reimburse their expenses, such as those incurred in converting foreign currency to U.S. dollars. You will, however, receive any dividends and other distributions in dollars. Your fees typically will be deducted from those dividends and distributions.

To say that ADRs have increased in popularity is something of an understatement. According to the Bank of New York, one of the leading issuers of ADRs, the dollar volume of all ADRs grew from $41 billion in 1988 to $503 billion in 2002, an increase of 1,127 percent in 11 years. That speaks volumes about the power of going global.

Scoring:

Because a), b), and c) are all vehicles for investing in foreign markets or companies, d) is the correct answer and is worth 4 points. This was a gift—consider it your first coup in international investing!

	Scoring for Chapter 5	
	Highest Possible Score	**Your Score**
Question 1	4	_____
Question 2	2	_____
Question 3	4	_____
Question 4	4	_____
Question 5	4	_____
CHAPTER TOTALS	18	_____

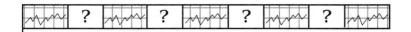

6 Portfolio Design— Diversification Works!

A classic mistake of many investors is to shoot for the quick score by loading up on the hot stock or sector du jour. We saw this happen during the technology boom of the last few years of the 20th century. Many investors rode the tech elevator to the penthouse, only to come crashing down to the sub-subbasement when that segment of the economy tanked. They lost all their gains and perhaps some of their principal as well; many still are wondering what hit them.

The culprit was failure to diversify their holdings. In investing, *diversification* means spreading your holdings among different asset classes to protect against sharp declines in certain investment categories. Diversified assets work as a team for you because they often have what people in the financial value call low "correlation coefficients."

Here's a concrete example: Suppose that during the tech boom, you purchased shares of both a microchip manufacturer and a telecommunications start-up—different types of business, but still both within the broad tech sector. On the surface, there seems no relation between these two companies or your investments in them. But companies within sectors tend to respond to the same macro forces, whether they are political instability, consumer pessimism, inflation, or other powerful movements. So all the companies in a certain sector may rise or fall together. If your investments are clustered within only one sector, all your stocks could tumble at once. And this may happen even though the companies in which you've invested have no seeming relationship.

When you listen to the daily stock market report, you'll get further evidence of how companies within sectors often move together. Do you notice that the announcer provides reports on the movements that day of utilities, transportation companies, and interest-sensitive stocks? That's because companies within these sectors tend to move up or down as a group, although the actual share prices within the sector also will reflect the differing values of the individual companies.

Undiversified portfolios represent risk. You can avoid that risk by diversifying your portfolio, selecting assets that don't correlate highly with each other. Often, uncorrelated assets will move in opposite directions; sometimes, they'll move in the same direction, but for different reasons. Holding uncorrelated assets may not bring you killer gains over the short term, but it will tend to smooth out the bumps over the long haul.

Consider again our example of investors who loaded up on tech stocks and paid a steep price for it. Let's suppose those same investors had divided their holdings over tech stocks, Blue Chip companies, and mutual funds that specialize in well-developed countries overseas. Our investment group still would have taken a hit in the tech sector, but their blue-chippers wouldn't have fared as badly because these old-line graybeards don't necessarily correlate highly with young tech businesses. As for the money invested in foreign-targeted mutual funds, that might have emerged unscathed, because markets overseas tend to respond to different forces than do domestic technology companies. This could be said: Same amount invested, much softer landing.

Fund managers spend long hours trying to select the most diversified portfolios they can, applying often complicated mathematical analyses and calculations to determine correlation values between assets and among asset classes. We won't get into the formulas in substantial detail here, but our questions this chapter will introduce you to some diversification principles and strategies. These should help you diversify your portfolio; or frame the right questions of your financial advisor or fund manager.

Question 1—

Which of these is not a major class of assets?

a) Cash assets.

b) Fixed-income assets.

c) Mutual fund assets.

d) Equity assets.

To achieve portfolio diversification, some investors purchase stocks of companies that operate in different sectors of the economy. That can work, yet there's a much more fundamental way of achieving a diversified portfolio—spreading your holdings through the different major categories of assets. Each of the categories has different risk and growth factors, and each responds differently to macroeconomic forces. The factors that drive one category down may have little or no impact on the other categories. This means your risk is reduced when you allocate your investments over several categories.

Cash assets are the category we've understood at some level since we first opened passbook savings accounts all those years ago. These assets aren't literally in cash, but they provide immediate access for us so we can convert them to cash. Checking and savings accounts are examples of cash assets, as are money market funds. If you sew your cash into a pillowcase, you're creating a cash asset of sorts.

Cash assets present little or no growth opportunity. Beyond the minimal interest that you may collect on your accounts, your principal will remain essentially unchanged. That's also the good news of cash assets—your principal will remain essentially unchanged, so there's no chance you'll lose it due to economic volatility.

While your principal is safe, cash assets *do* pose risks. If you deposit $1,000 in your pillowcase and leave it there for 10 years, you'll still have $1,000 when you slice open your homemade bank. Over those 10 years, however, inflation may have taken a nasty toll, significantly reducing the buying power of your $1,000. Your investment was safe; its purchasing power was at risk. We'll talk more about risk in Chapter 9.

Fixed-income assets introduce elements of both growth and risk. Among the most popular fixed-income assets are certificates of deposit and bonds. With each, you invest your money for a specified period in return for a prearranged interest payment. You enjoy greater growth than you would with cash assets, and in some cases the risks are minimized. With CDs, for example, the Federal Deposit Insurance Corporation (FDIC) insures your accounts. Typically, the FDIC protects up to $100,000 in total assets deposited with, or held through, a single financial institution.

Bonds, however, increase the risk factor. Bonds are issued by corporations, the federal government, and state and local governments to raise capital for a broad range of tasks. For corporations, bonds often help underwrite expansion. For governments, bonds can finance a variety of improvements to parks and roadways or other civic ventures. Bonds are typically long-term investments (the maturity period can be as along as 30 years) that offer what appear to be guaranteed interest payments above the return of your principal.

Each bond is backed by "the full faith and credit" of the issuing entity. Sometimes that's protection enough, but there are times when it isn't. When Enron and Adelphia experienced severe economic difficulties, for example, the ramifications included default of scheduled bond interest payments. Bondholders were left wondering if they ever would see their principal again, much less interest payments; in such cases, bondholders may receive only "cents-on-the-dollar" value for their holdings once the smoke clears.

Government default on bond payments is rarer, but the infrequency of the occurrence didn't salve the pain of Orange County, California, investors when that government couldn't make its bond payments some years ago. History shows us that in the area of defaults, if it can happen, it will happen.

On the high side of both risk and reward are equity investments, most commonly stocks. With these, you actually acquire an ownership interest—usually a tiny piece—of the entity issuing the stock. Unlike cash assets, stocks offer no assurances that your principal will be safe; all of it is at risk. Unlike fixed-income assets, equity assets offer no guaranteed interest payments; your return depends on the performance of your stocks in the market.

But also unlike cash or fixed-income assets, equity assets don't limit your upside potential. Both your risk and your profit potential are considerable. That's why equity investments are at once alluring and potentially dangerous.

(Mutual funds, by the way, are not a major asset category. Such funds can include stocks, bonds, or both, so they're best thought of as an investment subclass. Subclasses will be covered in Question 2.)

Once you understand the major asset classes, you'll have a better idea of how to allocate your investments to provide growth potential and some protection against principal loss. You wouldn't want to salt everything away in cash assets where there's no upside potential. On the other hand, you might not want to dump everything into the stock market because your entire investment would be at risk. Spreading assets among the classes can produce a diversified portfolio for you.

Moreover, your diversification formula need not be static. If you anticipate a period of growth for the stock market, for example, you may decide to shift a greater percentage of your portfolio to stocks. If you detect a market slump on the horizon, you can do the reverse: Sell some stocks and invest the proceeds in cash assets, even if you see that as no more than a temporary parking space.

Maintaining a diversified portfolio is a dynamic process that involves both research and a willingness to shift funds. It's a vital part of portfolio management.

Scoring:

Since major asset classes don't include mutual funds, score 4 points for c), 0 for any other answer.

Question 2—

Which of these is not a subclass of fixed-income assets?

a) Treasury bills.

b) Intermediate Treasury bonds.

c) Small-Cap stocks.

d) Long-term Treasury notes.

Knowing the major asset classes is a great start on diversifying your portfolio. Within the major classes, however, are subclasses of investments, each with its own characteristic risk and return factors. In some cases, the differences are significant. Here are some of the most popular investment subclasses in the major category of fixed-income assets:

Treasury Bills.

T-bills, as they're commonly known, are loans from you to the U.S. Treasury Department. They carry a maturity of up to one year and offer a return that is all but risk-proof—the federal government would have to default for you not to realize the promised return. You pay for that assurance with a return that is relatively modest. In his book *Asset Allocation—Balancing Financial Risk,* Roger C. Gibson notes that the average compound rate of return for T-bills between 1925 and 1998 was 3.8 percent, barely outpacing the average inflation rate of 3.1 percent for the same period.

Intermediate-Term (5-Year) Treasury Notes.

These are similar to T-bills but with longer maturity periods. As with T-bills, you incur very little risk to your principal but your return could have a hard time keeping up with inflation.

Long-Term (20-year) Treasury Bonds.

Another government vehicle with a lengthy maturity term. Again, there's little risk of default but some chance that inflation will erode your gains and then some. In his book *The Intelligent Asset Allocator,* William Bernstein indicates that long-term treasuries produced losses, once inflation was factored in, in 20 of the 73 years between 1925 and 1998.

Corporate Bonds.

As previously noted, corporations issue bonds to raise capital from investors, and they pledge a specific return for the privilege. The rewards can be greater than with government-issued vehicles, but as we've seen, so too are the risks.

Generally, corporate bonds can be considered high-quality or high-yield bonds; they're rated along that continuum by such services as Standard & Poor's and Moody's. High-yield bonds, sometimes called by the unflattering nickname "junk bonds," pay greater interest than do high-quality bonds, but they also bring the attendant risk of payment interruptions or default. Most companies honor their obligations most of the time, but a little analysis on your part can lead you to the red flags.

We know that both types of bonds are influenced by interest rate changes; high-yield bonds respond to general economic conditions as well. They may perform poorly in a sluggish economy for fear that companies strapped for cash will miss interest payments or even default.

There are other subclasses of fixed-income assets and different ways to package them—mutual funds, unit trusts, and insurance company products to cite a few. The key to success in this asset class is to understand the risks involved. This asset class is conservative; it most definitely is not risk-free.

The major class of equity assets also has important subclasses. Among them are:

Large-Cap Stocks.

We're used to thinking of stocks as an undifferentiated group, but those in the financial industry tend to divide them into three groups: large cap, mid cap, and small cap. ("Cap" refers to the value of the company's market capitalization.) A firm with capitalization of $5 billion or more is considered large-cap.

Some other observers use only two subcategories: large-company stocks—companies included in the S&P 500 exchange are commonly considered the large-company group—and small-company stocks. Bernstein indicates that from 1925 to 1998, the large-company group produced an average annual inflation-adjusted return of more than 8 percent. But you need a strong constitution to weather the down years. During the Great Depression, for example, the value of large-company stocks plummeted by almost two-thirds.

Mid-Cap Stocks.

Businesses with market capitalization between $1 billion and $5 billion are in this subcategory.

Small-Cap Stocks.

Those with market capitalization less than $1 billion are small-cap. If you're using the two-category scheme, companies in the bottom 20 percent of the New York Stock Exchange, as measured by outstanding stock value, are small-company stocks. But don't call them bottom-feeders. During that period from 1925 to 1998, these guys outperformed their larger cousins, producing an average annual inflation-adjusted return of greater than 9 percent, according to Bernstein. The risks were commensurate, as small-company stocks lost more than 85 percent of their value during the Great Depression.

International Stocks.

The securities of foreign-based companies are in this subclass, which can be broken down even further according to the economic situation of the home country—well-developed, developing, or emerging.

Real Estate.

Some observers consider real estate a fourth major asset class, while others regard it as a subclass of equity assets.

However you classify it, it does involve equity, since you own a property or belong to an investment group that owns a property. Unlike stocks, real estate can have substantial acquisition and maintenance costs, and it can be much more difficult to liquidate than stocks—that's why some regard it as a separate asset class.

Clearly, each of these equity asset subclasses differs from the other subclasses in important ways. Yet another differentiation is whether they're "value" or "growth" assets. Investors interested in value assets search for stocks that represent good "value" relative to their price. A value-oriented investor is less likely to pay more, or much more, for a stock than its perceived current worth. Typically, value stocks have comparatively low price/earnings ratios.

Growth-oriented investors focus on companies that are projected to grow rapidly, with a commensurate increase in stock prices. These investors aren't terribly concerned about the price they're paying because they anticipate significant returns in short order. By nature, growth stocks tend to be riskier and more volatile on the upside and downside.

These two styles of investing come in and out of favor based on the economy and changes in the business cycle. There's no clear relationship between the two. Value stocks and growth stocks may rise or fall together, or they could move in opposite directions. Many well-balanced portfolios employ both approaches.

Armed with your knowledge of major asset classes and subclasses, you're ready to pursue a diversified portfolio. We tend to invest in those classes we know best. If you're familiar with all the classes, you can become a *multiple-class* investor. Over the long haul, multiple-class investors tend to achieve better performance than single-class investors because of the diversification of their portfolios.

Scoring:

Small-Cap stocks is a subclass of equity assets, not fixed-income assets. Therefore, Score 4 points for c), 0 for any other answer.

Question 3—

Which of these correlation coefficients for two asset classes will tend to yield the most diversified portfolio?

a) 0

b) -5

c) 1

d) 5

Familiarizing yourself with asset classes and subclasses will let you know what's out there. But how do you know which to select for your portfolio? How do you know which of these classes will have an inverse correlation—that is, which will rise when others fall to minimize the risk factor? You can try a conceptual approach, but it's pretty hard to deduce any relationship at all between, say, T-bills and real estate.

There is a more reliable approach that deploys what are known as *correlation coefficients*. It involves plugging actual returns of asset classes over a long period into a mathematical formula to determine the relationship between two (or more) asset classes. The result is expressed as a correlation coefficient.

Most financial advisors will have correlation coefficients for you or can easily determine them. Many subscription services routinely make them available. With the aid of software packages, you can figure out correlation coefficients yourself. Let's assume you want to develop the correlation coefficient for two asset classes or subclasses. Begin by listing the returns for each category over a lengthy period, say, 20 years. Then insert the numbers into your software package. The result will be the correlation coefficient for those two asset categories.

Correlation coefficients always lie between -1 and 1. A coefficient of 1 indicates that the groups are perfectly correlated; they tend to move up or down in tandem. When one experiences a big gain, so does the other. When one drops dramatically, so does the other.

A coefficient of -1 indicates a perfect inverse correlation—their movements are in opposite directions. When one soars, the other plunges. A coefficient of 0 indicates no correlation at all.

For the purposes of portfolio diversification and risk avoidance, the lower the correlation coefficient, the better. Holding uncorrelated, minimally correlated, or inversely correlated assets will serve as a buffer against dramatic losses in your portfolio. One of your asset sectors may weaken, but if your other holdings aren't correlated with that group, they may remain strong and help you avert disaster.

You can take this approach a step further to help you determine which individual stocks provide the best diversification. Let's suppose, for example, that you determine a weak correlation between T-bills and small-company stocks and that each class should be represented in your portfolio. But which small-company stocks should you purchase? You can go through the same mathematical process, this time inserting return data for the specific stocks you may be contemplating. This will produce a more individualized correlation coefficient, rather than a class-to-class coefficient.

Correlation coefficients are most useful in determining the performance relationship between asset classes or subclasses for which no relationship is immediately apparent. Bernstein, for example, ran the numbers on Japanese small-company stocks and domestic real estate investment trusts (REITs), each an asset subclass, and found no correlation between the two. Thus, these two subclasses can make a productive mix in a diversified portfolio, a conclusion that would be hard to reach with a conceptual approach to investing.

Scoring:

A coefficient of 0 would help assure portfolio diversification. Score 4 points for a), 0 for any other answer.

Question 4—

Which of these is the best description of *hedge fund*?

a) A fund that accepts minimal investments to protect against loss.

b) A fund that "hedges" its investments to provide diversification.

c) A fund that invests only in sure things.

d) A fund that invests in makers of garden supplies.

As we've seen, diversification is the primary goal of portfolio design. There are a number of approaches to diversification, including holding assets with low correlation coefficients to minimize risk. Hedge funds often take a different tack. These funds, which may involve stocks, bonds, or mutual funds,

111

often factor in correlation coefficients when purchasing assets. But many of them also hold both "long" and "short" positions in their assets.

Most of us are used to buying long, that is, we purchase assets in the hope that we'll make a profit when their values rise. Buying short is the reverse. When you buy short, you're actually selling the asset now, at its current value, and agreeing to purchase it a specified time in the future. If the asset declines in value, you sell it at the reduced value and make a profit on the difference between the high sale price and the lower purchase price.

Many investors regard short positions as *anathema*. To make money in short positions, asset values must decline, meaning that short holders must cheer for poor results from their companies. Championing failure doesn't sit well with many investors, so they eschew shorting altogether.

For hedge funds, though, it's an essential element of strategy. When they hold long and short positions—not in the same asset, of course—they know that they're protecting fund investors against principal loss. When the markets rise, they make money on their long positions. Should markets dive, they profit on their short positions.

This is a sophisticated strategy that even some hedge funds don't implement perfectly. Many are hedge funds in name only—they don't really hedge their bets. Before entering a hedge fund, it's a good idea to carefully examine their holdings to make sure investments really are hedged.

The ultimate portfolio, one that maximizes profits while minimizing risk, has been the holy grail of financial experts for years. Some believe they've found it, attributing its discovery to Harry Markowitz, widely hailed as the father of Modern Portfolio Theory.

According to Markowitz (as captured by Contingency Analysis, *www.contingencyanalysis.com*), you can reach the optimal portfolio this way. First, for any level of market risk, consider all the portfolios with that degree of volatility. From among that group, pick the portfolio that has the highest expected return. Or you can get at it the other way: For any expected return, consider all the portfolios with precisely that projected return. From that group, pick the one with the lowest volatility. *Voila!* Either way you approach the calculation, you come up with what Markowitz called the "Efficient Frontier," the alpha and omega of well-balanced portfolios.

To craft your ultimate portfolio as Markowitz suggests, you'll need precise data, including expected returns, volatilities, and correlation coefficients. That information will define the field from which you reach the Efficient Frontier, which actually includes a curve of optimal portfolios rather than a single magic bullet.

The ground-breaking theories of Markowitz and others today serve as a pillar of risk management for many major players, including banks and insurance companies that make their living by weighing investment risk. Markowitz shared a Nobel Prize in 1990 for his work in portfolio selection and corporate finance, further indication that portfolio diversification is serious business.

Scoring:

> Score 4 points for b), the best definition for hedge fund. Score 0 points for a) and c); the minimum investment for hedge funds can be quite high, and even hedge funds don't always select sure-fire winners. If you answered d), give yourself 1 point. We like your sense of humor.

	Scoring for Chapter 6	
	Highest Possible Score	**Your Score**
Question 1	4	_____
Question 2	4	_____
Question 3	4	_____
Question 4	4	_____
CHAPTER TOTALS	16	_____

7 Asset Allocation— The Right Division Means Multiplication

In the broadest sense, there are two approaches to investing. One strategy might be called market timing—trying to anticipate how markets will perform over the short term, then reacting appropriately, either by getting in when markets are about to take off or getting out when they're about to nose-dive.

This is the approach propagated by hundreds of subscription services and newsletters hawking their advice to unwary investors. People are so hungry for the right advice that they listen to these rent-a-gurus, who bring more art than science to market prognostications. Even if they develop comprehensive knowledge of the markets—and that's giving them the benefit of the doubt—who among them can foresee when a terrorist attack will level the World Trade Center towers, or when the collapse of a major company like Enron will send markets plummeting?

Cataclysmic events will happen, but no one can say just when. The gurus are quick to crow when they hit it right, but let's face it: Even a broken watch is right twice a day. For investors risking what may constitute their life savings, that may not be a persuasive success rate. Look at market timing another way. If the rent-a-gurus are successful market-timers, why aren't they filthy rich and retired to private Caribbean islands rather than hustling their wares to you?

Market timing is the quick-fix approach to investing; it simply doesn't work consistently. The bottom line on markets is that there are no definable trends or formulas for the short term. Market timing is a gamble, neither more nor less.

Asset allocation, the second broad approach to investing, is a strategy geared to the long term. It involves distributing investments across the entire spectrum of asset classes, carefully monitoring those investments, and rebalancing portfolios on a regular basis. It's easily enough stated, but asset allocation involves considerable education, research, and preparation.

To successfully deploy asset allocation, you must familiarize yourself with all asset classes, as well as the subclasses and sectors within those major categories, before you can choose the right assets for your portfolio and spread your investments among them. You'll need to get a firm handle on risk—not only the various types of risk, but also the risk-return relationship for each potential investment. Part of your preparation in asset allocation involves finding a risk level that's tolerable for you.

You'll also need to develop the proper psychological approach to asset allocation. This is a strategy for the long term; creating just the right mix of patience and action is a task that many investors find the most difficult of all, yet it's crucial to a successful asset-allocation approach.

In this scenario, the actual selection of the stock, bond, or mutual fund typically is the last step. Think of asset allocation as the investing equivalent of shopping for an important dinner party. You don't rush pell-mell to the supermarket and start tossing items frantically into your cart. Instead, you engage in research and planning first.

How many people will be coming? Who's on the guest list? Is it a sit-down affair or a buffet? Do any of your guests have special dietary concerns? Will hors d'oeuvres be part of the program? Once you've answered these fundamental questions, you're ready to rough out a menu and hit the grocery store. Not only will you be well-prepared to get every item you need, but your thorough preparation will allow you to compare prices and select the best value. That's the way individual asset selection works in the long-term approach. It's well-informed and orderly, and it relies on comprehensive planning.

In Chapter 6, we introduced you to diversification and the principles of Modern Portfolio Theory (MPT), which is based on the concept of multiple-class investing to reduce overall portfolio fluctuation. (By the way, did we mention that Harry Markowitz shared a Nobel Prize for his contributions to MPT? They don't give Nobels to market-timers.) Our next series of questions will dig into asset allocation, going beyond the theory to some of the most important practical considerations.

Question 1—

In investing, the term "standard deviation" is best defined as a measure of:

a) How far your portfolio differs from the Efficient Frontier.

b) The projected behavior of investors when their assets go south.

c) The difference in the values of assets in your portfolio.

d) The risk associated with various assets.

All investments bring risk; some investments are riskier than others; some investments are more risky than others over certain periods, less risky than others over certain periods. Standard deviation helps measure the risk of investment classes and subclasses, both now and over extended periods. Because standard deviation figures help quantify risk, they allow you to compare the risk of various investments and guide you to the optimum holding periods for those assets.

Always expressed as a percentage, the standard deviation tells you how far the value of an asset will vary from the mean. Two-thirds of the time, the annual return of the asset will fall between one standard deviation above and one standard deviation below the mean value of the asset. If you know the returns of the assets you're studying, you can insert the figures into a formula available through many software packages and calculate standard deviations yourself. Many online financial services provide standard deviation information, and it's pretty commonly offered by professional portfolio managers.

Calculating the figures yourself isn't as important as understanding what they mean. A high standard deviation—15 percent, for example—tells you that your asset is more volatile than many others, and that you're probably boarding a roller coaster. A low standard deviation suggests the reverse—that your asset is pretty stable and won't likely subject you to a wild ride.

But standard deviations are affected by the length of time assets are held. When Jeremy J. Siegel studied the standard deviations of stocks and bonds for his book *Stocks for the Long Run,* he found that when held for a one-year period, stocks are much more volatile and risky than bonds, with a standard deviation running about twice as high. By year 10 of the holding period, the difference in standard deviation between these two asset classes all but evaporates. By year 20, the standard deviation for bonds surpasses the measure for stocks.

This means that if you hold stocks for 20 years, they actually become less risky investments than bonds held for the same period. This might be contrary to our concept of fixed-income assets as much safer than equity assets, yet that's the influence of time on risk.

When we invest in the market, our biggest fear is that we will lose everything. This happens, but rarely. A more likely occurrence is that volatility over time will erode our profits and perhaps cut into our principal. It's this "market risk," as those in the industry call it, that's the ever-present danger, more subtle than a complete wipeout because it takes place over time. Standard deviation figures will give you a sense of the volatility of asset classes and individual stocks and bonds, enabling you to match your growth expectations with your risk tolerance.

Scoring:

> Standard deviation is a measure of volatility or risk, so d) is the best answer here. Score 4 points for d), 0 for any other answer.

Question 2—

In diversifying your portfolio, it's best to invest in:

a) One class of assets.

b) Two classes of assets.

c) Three classes of assets.

d) Four classes of assets (including real estate).

In investing, the whole often is greater than the sum of its parts. Thus, if you spread your investments over as many asset classes as possible, history shows that your holdings as a group are likely to outperform any of the individual investments.

When Roger C. Gibson undertook a longitudinal study of multiple-class investing for his book *Asset Allocation—Balancing Financial Risk,* he was able to flesh out the safety-in-numbers theory. Examining the period from 1972 to 1998, he found that portfolios featuring four asset classes outperformed those with three asset classes; three-asset-class portfolios did better than those with two asset classes, which themselves produced greater returns than single-asset portfolios. The figures in this study show clearly that the more asset classes you include, the greater your return is likely to be over time.

These results were mirrored in the category of volatility/risk. Four-asset-class portfolios experienced less volatility than those with three asset classes, and so on down the line. In fact, single-asset portfolios had a standard deviation nearly twice as high as those with four asset categories, underscoring the heightened risks that come with undiversified holdings.

Allocation models and the amount you invest in major assets classes and subclasses should be based on your goals and risk tolerance. For example, a conservative investor with the objective of asset accumulation could adopt this allocation:

- ◻ 60% Fixed Income, including:

  - ▪ 20% High-Yield Corporate Bonds.

  - ▪ 20% Corporate Bonds.

  - ▪ 20% Government Bonds.

- ◻ 40% Equity, including:

  - ▪ 10% International Stocks.

  - ▪ 10% Real Estate.

  - ▪ 20% U.S. Stocks.

On the other hand, an aggressive investor with the same goal might implement this allocation:

- ▣ 20% Fixed-Income, including:

  - 10% High-Yield Corporate Bonds.

  - 10% Government Bonds.

- ▣ 80% Equity, including:

  - 20% International Stocks.

  - 20% Real Estate.

  - 40% U.S. Stocks.

As you consider all the factors in portfolio design, you can balance even more precisely, for example, dividing your International Stocks allocation between companies in well-developed nations and those in emerging markets. A well-balanced portfolio can be as elementary or as sophisticated as you need it to be, but it must be consistent with your tolerance for risk. During the bear market that began in March 2000, many who had considered themselves aggressive investors got queasy and pulled out—missing the ensuing recovery. If your risk tolerance is low, a conservative portfolio may be the way to go.

Before you adopt the "more asset classes are better" theory as a guiding principle, keep several caveats in mind. First, this approach can work for you if the subclasses of assets you choose are not strongly correlated. It won't do you much good to select multiple asset classes if you end up investing in assets that move up or down together, despite belonging to different major classes. An important part of designing multiple-asset-class portfolios is checking out the correlation coefficients of assets within the portfolio and understanding the potential impact of macro forces and other factors on the asset classes you select.

Also, remember that the results Gibson noted occurred over an extended period of time. In a given year, perhaps even over a several-year period, any asset class or subclass may experience a dizzying ride up or a precipitous plunge. If you consider only this brief period, your comparative performances may be quite different, and you might be tempted to consider a single-asset-class portfolio. But remember the risk you take when you do so. Over time, investing in multiple asset classes lowers risk and, as Gibson's figures show, can produce higher returns.

Finally, it must be recognized that investing in multiple asset classes usually means putting your faith and cash in assets with which you may not be familiar. Many of us stick with what we know, or what we *think* we know—usually large-company stocks—rather than climb the slippery slopes of foreign-targeted mutual funds or real estate investment trusts. It's natural to want to exercise caution in areas where we have little experience or expertise.

But instead of dismissing asset categories because you're not familiar with them, *get* familiar with them. Chances are you'll need them to design the ultimate portfolio for you.

Scoring:

Score 4 points for d), 0 for any other answer.

Question 3—

The optimum holding period for stocks is:

a) 5 years.

b) 10 years.

c) 15 years.

d) None of the above is necessarily the optimum holding period.

Because media often hype dramatic gains or losses in high-profile stocks, equity investments often appear to us to be the riskiest asset class. Over the short term, this can be true. But when you invest for the long term, stocks not only become less risky in an absolute sense, but they become less risky than other asset categories—particularly cash assets and fixed-income assets, whose modest returns can be eaten up by inflation.

Siegel investigated the long-term performance of asset classes and found that, for every 20-year period since 1802, the returns provided by bonds and Treasury bills didn't keep pace with inflation. Stocks, on the other hand, never fell behind inflation when 20-year holding periods were considered. In fact, if investors stuck with the stock market for at least 17 years, they never experienced a negative return for the entire holding period, even with inflation factored in.

(Note that we're not recommending that you hang on to individual stocks for that entire period. Clearly, regular portfolio maintenance means liquidating some issues and acquiring others. Rather, the positive returns Siegel cites are achieved by remaining in the market generally for those lengthy periods.)

If stocks provide a superior return over the long haul, why is it that some investors switch asset categories as routinely as others change socks? The answer might lie in the psychology of investors.

For one thing, many investors can't envision being in any category of investment for 20 years. Two decades is too long a time frame for many to contemplate. If that describes you, look at it this way. Should you begin funding a 401(k) plan or individual retirement account when you're 30, you may be investing in that plan for as long as 40 years or so before you begin taking distributions. That's a major-league time frame, giving you the opportunity to fashion an effective asset-allocation approach to your account.

Even if you've retired without undertaking any significant investing, you still can plan for the long term. The lengthening of life spans in the United States has seen to that. According to the U.S. Census Bureau, men who turned 65 in the year 2000 can expect to live, on average, another 16.3 years; women who celebrated their 65th birthdays in 2000 can look forward to 19.2 more years, on average. For you, a long-term investing strategy to create wealth for you and your heirs still makes sense.

The need for immediate gratification is another element in the psychological make-up of investors that tends to discourage long-term planning. When our financial advisors tell us that a stock mutual fund averages 10 percent annual return, we blank out on the word "average" and expect that 10 percent return every year. When we don't get it, we're disheartened, panicked, or both.

Our resolve may be further weakened by media reports of dramatic fluctuations in stock market prices. Media tend to focus on short-term performance; when the pundits tell us that one of our asset classes is on the express elevator going down, we feel the irresistible urge to shift our money to an asset category that, for the moment, is faring better.

This uneasy feeling can be exacerbated by the inevitable disasters—natural and otherwise—throughout the world. Hostilities erupt, crops and companies fail, CEOs and auditors go to jail—all these calamities will have a significant short-term impact on stocks and, if we overreact, propel us to other asset classes. Think about it for a moment. Has there ever been a period without such stomach-churning disasters? Can't name one, and yet stocks invariably outperform other asset classes over the long term.

It's almost always the case that one sector or asset class will be performing better than another, and that the lagger will appear a loser that we should abandon. Financial professionals have a name for this phenomenon—chasing performance— and it's almost always a formula for failure.

Instead of chasing performance, stick to your game plan. It takes nerve and resolve to do it in the face of discouraging short-term trends. History shows you'll be a winner over time.

All that having been said, it must be acknowledged that there is no real optimal holding period for stocks. Generally speaking, for an asset-allocation approach to yield the best results, the longer you're in the market steadily, the better. You also may have short-term objectives for which you've invested, goals that may require liquidation of assets and the taking of profits now.

Suppose you're investing to raise money for a new car or a down payment for a house. It makes little sense to consider a 20-year holding period for your stocks; you want your ride or your domicile long before then. If this investment is the only one in your portfolio, you *will* be out of the market for awhile.

These exceptions notwithstanding, it makes sense to plan for the long term. Don't be swayed by bad news today. If you stick to your guns, you'll likely have plenty of good news tomorrow.

Scoring:

> The best answer is d), since optimal holding periods depend on the goals of each investor. Score 4 points for d). However, since longer holding periods for equity assets generally are better rewarded, score 2 points for c) and 1 point for b).

Question 4—

Which of these statements most accurately describes the best investing schedule:

a) There is no single schedule that's best for all investors.

b) Allocate the same percentage of your money each month until you've invested all the money you've designated for this purpose.

c) Invest all available money now.

d) Time your investments to asset performance, striking when the price is best.

Once you fashion the ultimate portfolio for your needs and determine what percentage of your funds to allocate to each asset, you must decide how to schedule your investments. If you're managing your own portfolio, your investment schedule will be up to you. But if you're working with an outside portfolio manager, many experts suggest that any actual investing be preceded by formation of an investment policy statement (IPS).

For institutional fund managers, an IPS, or its equivalent, is often a legal requirement. That may not be the case for you, but if you and your portfolio manager develop a statement that outlines your financial goals, your asset allocation formula, your investment schedule, and the parameters for portfolio review and modification, you'll both have a clear understanding of your goals and methods of operation. You'll proceed from a shared vision, and you'll be less prone to knee-jerk reactions and second-guessing.

Even if you're handling your investment matters yourself, it's not a bad idea to rough out an IPS. Having a concrete statement of your goals and methodology may keep you from making emotional investment decisions. And if you ever do engage an outside advisor, your IPS will be ready to roll.

With your IPS in hand, you're ready to schedule your investments. Committing the entire nest egg is one approach, but that would give many investors pause; they're reluctant to commit all their money until they see some evidence of performance. This is a natural concern, and there are alternatives.

One is to invest the same amount regularly—every month, for example—in a given asset, a technique known as dollar cost averaging (DCA). In most cases, the value of the target asset will change over your entire investment period. When the value is higher, your investment will purchase fewer shares; when the value drops, your investment buys more shares. Because you're buying more shares at a lower price, you actually may end up with a lower per-share cost than if you had invested all your money at once. DCA doesn't always bring that happy outcome, but it's often psychologically more acceptable to investors than the "Big Bang" approach.

Another method of gradual investing, developed by Michael Edleson, is called value averaging (VA). It involves investing only enough each month to achieve the desired total value of your account or portfolio. Let's suppose that your goal is to achieve an account balance of $2,400 after two years. Assuming no growth in your account, you would need to invest $100 each month to reach your goal. So you begin with an initial investment of $100 in Month 1.

Here's where the mechanics of VA kick in. In Month 2, you invest whatever it takes to give you an account balance of $200. In Month 3, your goal is total value of $300, so you invest whatever amount will bring you up to $300. You determine each month's investment in the same manner.

Through the life of your two-year investment program, you actually may need to produce less than $2,400 because any growth in your account will mean that a smaller investment is required to reach your monthly goal. But the reverse also is true. If your account balance declines, you'll need to invest more than you had planned to reach the desired objective.

As dollar cost averaging, VA is not a panacea. It assures that you will end up with no more than you originally projected, though it may cost you less to get there. If you take that same hypothetical $2,400 and invest it all now, you could achieve a balance well above your original investment. Yet VA is a schedule of gradual investing that appeals to many investors, particularly those trying the market for the first time.

The bottom line on investment scheduling is that one size does not fit all. If you've designed a good-looking portfolio, go ahead and invest on a schedule that's within your comfort zone.

Scoring:

The best answer, worth 4 points, is a), since investors should determine the schedules that best suit them. If you answered b) or c)—both credible scheduling strategies—score 2 points. If your answer is d), you get 0 points. This is a market-timing approach that's fraught with peril.

	Scoring for Chapter 7	
	Highest Possible Score	**Your Score**
Question 1	4	_____
Question 2	4	_____
Question 3	4	_____
Question 4	4	_____
CHAPTER TOTALS	16	_____

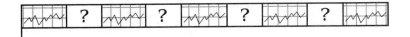

8

The Figs—
Study Them Carefully

When you commit to a philosophy of diversification reflected in selection of multiple asset classes, you're building a solid foundation for success. But the individual assets you choose for your portfolio play a key role as well. We know that being in the stock market continuously over a considerable period is the best way to maximize growth and reduce risks in this asset class. Yet which securities should you pick? Because the performance of stocks varies widely, your purchase decisions are vital. The financial industry has developed a number of ways to measure the performance of individual issues—we'll focus on these tools in this chapter.

Before we do, let's again review the two broad approaches to investing in the stock market: investing and speculating. While the stock market can be used for both, the investor uses the market to achieve long-term growth, knowing that equity investments can provide a greater return than fixed-income assets. Investors understand that their gains will occur over time, even though the individual stocks in their portfolios will experience good years and bad. They know that at the end of the day, their well-chosen stocks or mutual funds will outperform fixed-income assets, and that they diminish their risk by sticking with the program.

Speculators, on the other hand, are now-oriented, market-timers who shoot for the big score today while disdaining the risks of such high-stakes rolling. Speculating is not based on the fundamental principles—earnings, debt load, and so on—that investors review and analyze before making their purchase and sell decisions.

This doesn't mean that speculators don't score. They can, and they can score big. Witness the initial success of Internet and technology stocks during the late 1990s. But speculators are oblivious to the risks of their approach. When the tech market tanked, many of them lost their profits and much of their principal, a vivid illustration of one of Murphy's Laws of Investing: *Inordinate risk always precedes inordinate calamity.*

Speculating is not the gut-churning style that most of us would prefer. The alternative is to become a knowledgeable investor, one who studies the fundamentals and makes rational buy-sell decisions. Our next series of questions will test your expertise in this area, and help you fill any information gaps.

Question 1—

Which of these commodities or sectors was the object of the first documented speculative frenzy in market history?

a) Railroad stocks.

b) Tulips.

c) Steel stocks.

d) Internet stocks.

Financial frenzy is nothing new. In the late 19th century, railroad stocks were the object of considerable speculation. Created in 1894, the Rail Index is the oldest in the United States and the forerunner of today's Dow Jones Transportation Average. There was at least some logic to the speculation since much of the industrial base for America's great growth spurt was still being formalized in corporate shape, so there weren't many corporate stocks.

Railroads outperformed industrial stocks every year between 1900 and 1902, when a combination of the gathering strength of industrials and an economic downturn known as the *Rich Man's Panic* ended forever the dominance of rail stocks as a speculative medium.

Railroads continued to be important to the American economy—not as an independent sector but as one of the driving forces in industrial growth. We saw this pattern repeated in our own time in the unrestrained rush to the securities of Internet companies—and subsequent widespread losses when the bubble burst. Even as many Internet companies failed and took their speculators along with them, those that survived helped strengthen Old Economy companies by improving the technology components of their operations.

Speculation in rail stocks proved a fertile breeding ground for an attendant scandal—dubious accounting practices. In his 1920 book *The Value of a Railroad Security,* Floyd W. Mundy bemoaned the inability of shareholders to get honest numbers from the rails in which they had invested.

"Even with financial statements...keen discrimination is still necessary because financial statements are by no means proof against juggling," Mundy warned. "When a large corporation presents a statement involving the financial accounts of numerous subsidiaries, it is difficult even for an accountant to get beneath the surface. There are innumerable ways in which assets can be concealed or inflated as desired, and it is obviously impossible for the average investor or speculator to get much more real information than the management wishes to give out."

It's as if Mundy were gazing into a crystal ball to predict our own Enron and WorldCom accounting scandals. He even used the terms *old economy* to describe America's pre-industrial past and *new economy* as the shorthand for its industry-centered present. Apparently not much has changed in the past eight decades.

What Mundy knew is that speculative frenzies are all alike, attracting investors to some phenomenon that will "change the paradigm." No matter the commodity, stocks, or technology at the center of frenzies, they involve irrational decisions based on unreasonable and never-realized profit expectations, the leveraging of real assets to acquire the speculative properties, and a subsequent crash that leaves most craze participants high and dry. Yet in odd and thoroughly unanticipated ways, hysteria can strengthen the existing economy, entirely apart from its projected merits.

Such was the case with the earliest known speculative frenzy, which engulfed the seemingly stolid folks of The Netherlands in the 17th century. It was based on the innocuous bulb plant of the lily family, the tulip.

"The euphoric episode," writes John Kenneth Galbraith in his book *A Short History of Financial Euphoria,* "is protected and sustained by the will of those who are involved, in order to justify the circumstances that are making them rich. And it is equally protected by the will to ignore, exorcise, or condemn those who express doubts."

Tulipomania began innocently enough, Galbraith recounts, shortly after the first of the flowers was imported to Holland in the mid-16th century. At first, the bulbs were appreciated for their beauty and decorative value. But when people began to see profits in the plants, the frenzy began.

Speculators mortgaged their properties and sold convertible assets to acquire capital for tulip purchases. Tulip exchange markets were established in Amsterdam, Rotterdam, and other cities great and small across Holland. The fever was so high that by 1636, a single bulb might fetch a price of 3,000 florins— $25,000 to $50,000 today.

Presented with the chance to hop aboard a runaway speculative train, a veteran investor will ask hard questions: Is there a sustainable market for the product? Is it priced appropriately? Is supply commensurate with demand? Are distribution channels adequate? And finally, can current levels of profitability be maintained? But in a speculative frenzy, rationality is the first casualty, and that was the case with Tulipomania.

It wasn't long before the bloom was off the tulip. In 1637, tulips wilted. Many investors never made a profit and lost all the solid assets they had sold or leveraged to underwrite their hapless adventures.

"The wise and the nervous began to detach," Galbraith writes, "no one knows for what reason; others saw them go; the rush to sell became a panic; the prices dropped as if over a precipice."

Tulipomania sent Holland into an economic tailspin that lasted for years. It became a classic model for speculative frenzies: A commodity, sector, or group of stocks becomes wildly popular for reasons that defy apparent logic and the conventional laws of sustainability; a few speculators get in early, take huge profits and exit the frenzy filthy rich; most speculators lose their gains and much of their principal because they don't get out before reason prevails again.

Lest you think that Tulipomania was the product of some never-to-be-repeated 17th century quirkiness, substitute the words *Internet stocks* for *tulips*, and you'll find the scenario was replayed. Participants in the Internet frenzy jumped into a panicked market without asking tough questions about profitability, briefly realized gains, then lost them and more in the return to earth. When the tech sector plummeted, the impact of the crash on the overall economy was hauntingly similar to the disastrous effect of the plunge in tulips.

Speculative frenzies don't change much. Their enduring irony is that they *do* bring benefits. Holland emerged from Tulipomania a chastened community, but one with a renewable, viable tulip industry that, once the echoes of the frenzy had quieted, grew famously to become a much-loved symbol of a nation. The dust from our own dot-com debacle is still settling, but when it does, we may be left with a core of innovative, successful companies that are the driving force of an important new information industry—and a vehicle for improvement of Old Economy stalwarts.

A lucky few survive speculative frenzies; fewer still are those who prosper and go on to purchase private islands and NBA franchises. There are better, less risky ways to approach the market.

Scoring:
Score 4 points for b), 0 for any other answer.

Question 2—

Which of these is not a required filing of publicly held companies in America?

a) Balance Sheet.

b) Income Statement.

c) Statement of Cash Flow.

d) Statement of Income Projections.

Investors interested in long-term growth and risk avoidance don't speculate. Rather, they study the financial statements of potential investment targets to determine their growth prospects. Public companies in the United States are held to a series of quarterly filings that provide information over a broad variety of categories; all this information is readily available to you, and all of it can guide you in your investment decisions. Reading these documents isn't hard. Understanding their implications can be a bit trickier.

Balance sheets (Figure 8-1 on page 136) are perhaps the most rudimentary of the documents, indicating assets (what the business owns), and liabilities(what the business owes).

"Think of them," advises *The Motley Fool Investment Workbook,* from which a number of the following definitions are drawn, "as a snapshot of a company's underlying financial situation, with everything reflected, from cash to heavy equipment, from office desks to business travel costs."

On balance sheets, assets typically are divided into two subcategories. *Current assets* include everything that can be converted to cash quickly, such as money in bank accounts, T-bills, and money market accounts, and any associated interest payments. Also included are accounts receivable—payments that have been billed but not yet collected—and inventory, no matter what stage it might be in.

The other category of assets is called *fixed assets.* Here we find property, equipment, and machinery—all vital holdings for successful companies but none of them easily convertible to cash.

Liabilities similarly come in two flavors. *Short-term liabilities* are debts, such as licensing payments and debts to suppliers, which must be satisfied within one year. *Long-term liabilities* are those that extend beyond the next 12 months, including long-term debt that must be paid down over a fixed schedule.

Many balance sheets also feature a section called *stockholders' equity* or *shareholders' equity,* which shows what assets the company would hold if all short-term debts and long-term liabilities were settled now. In his work on balance sheets, Leopold A. Bernstein calls stockholders' equity the "residual rewards" of ownership. Typical line items in the stockholders'

Company XYZ
Balance Sheet
December XX, 20XX

ASSETS
CURRENT ASSETS

Cash	55,000	
Accounts Receivable	30,000	
Inventory	48,000	
		133,000

FIXED ASSETS

Leasehold Improvements	15,000	
Equipment	8,500	
Furniture and Fixtures	3,000	
	26,500	
Less: Accumulated Depreciation	(5,500)	
		21,000
TOTAL ASSETS		**154,000**

LIABILITIES AND STOCKHOLDERS' EQUITY
SHORT-TERM LIABILITIES

Line of Credit	15,000	
Current Portion of Notes Payable	10,000	
Accounts Payable	25,000	
Accrued Liabilities	2,000	
		52,000

LONG-TERM LIABILITIES

Notes Payable	35,000	
Less: Current portion	(10,000)	
		25,000

STOCKHOLDERS' EQUITY

Capital Stock - $1 par value, 10,000 shares authorized, 10,000 issued and outstanding	10,000	
Paid in Capital	15,000	
Retained Earnings	52,000	
		77,000
TOTAL LIABILITIES AND STOCKHOLDERS' EQUITY		**154,000**

Figure 8-1. Company XYZ Balance Sheet.

equity section include *paid in capital,* which indicates funds contributed to the corporation without the issuance of additional stock, and *retained earnings*—corporate net income not yet distributed to stockholders. The sum of stockholders' equity and total liabilities always equals total assets.

If you compare assets to liabilities, you get a sense of the financial "balance" of the company. Balance sheets give you a feel for the current financial position of companies, how well they're poised to progress. Income statements give you a better look at the here-and-now of company operations. Typical income statements—such as Figure 8-2 on page 138—will offer these line items:

- ◙ **Revenue,** the financial industry's term for gross sales. This will include all the money the company took in from sales, but it won't include any interest income. That's a separate line item.

- ◙ **Cost of Sales.** The direct costs for raw materials and the labor to fashion them into the company's goods.

- ◙ **Gross Profit.** If you subtract the cost of sales from revenues, you get a measure called *gross profit,* a line item on income statements.

- ◙ **Operating Expenses.** We've accounted for raw materials and production costs in the cost of sales category. Now we consider such other expenses as *Selling/General/Administration (SG&A)* and *Research and Development (R&D).*

- ◙ **Total Income Before Taxes.** To get this figure, subtract operating expenses from gross profit. Do you see what the income statement is doing? It's stating revenues, then subtracting costs by major category to arrive at a true profit figure—and show all the factors involved.

- ◙ **Income Taxes.** The total is listed here.

- ▣ **Net Income.** When income taxes are subtracted from total income before taxes, you arrive at net income, also known as earnings or profit. When you hear people refer to the "bottom line," net income is the figure they're most often referencing.

Company XYZ Income Statement as of December XX, 20XX		
REVENUE	350,000	
COST OF SALES	150,000	
GROSS PROFIT		200,000
OPERATING EXPENSES		
SELLING/GENERAL AND ADMINISTRATIVE	115,000	
RESEARCH AND DEVELOPMENT	65,000	
		180,000
TOTAL INCOME BEFORE INCOME TAXES		20,000
INCOME TAXES		(5,000)
NET INCOME		15,000

Figure 8-2. Company XYZ Income Statement.

To help introduce you to income statements, the example in Figure 8-2 is a stripped-down version. In actual documents, you might find these categories as well:

- ▣ **Interest Income.** In this category is any income generated from interest-bearing vehicles. Interest income is a component of total income before taxes.

- ▣ **Earnings Per Share.** The "bottom line" isn't necessarily the final line on most income statements. Beneath it, we sometimes find earnings per share. To get it, you divide net income by the number of shares outstanding.

▣ **Shares Outstanding.** This figure, often the final entry, tells you the total number of the company's shares held by all parties, from the tiniest account to the most powerful institutional investor.

Except for earnings per share, figures on income statements typically are listed in thousands; when you see a net income figure written as 15,000, you must multiply it by 1,000 to get the actual net profit total of 15 million. (For some reason, most income statements disdain dollar signs.) Negative performance is shown within parentheses, so if a company experiences a negative net income of 10 million, this would appear as (10,000), rather than -10 million.

Publicly held companies file income statements quarterly, so you can review performance for any three-month period as well as for the entire year. Most companies also provide data for the past several years along with their current income statements.

Some income statements will have still other categories. For example, a business that acquires another company during the year may have line items for *Revenues from Continuing Operations* and a corresponding category for *Operating Expenses for Continuing Operations,* backing out the sales and costs for the newly purchased business. Nonrecurring costs may be footnoted and excluded from the categories to which they ordinarily would belong. Generally, though, income statements all include the information described above, with line items that are fairly consistent.

Once you have the data from the income statement, you can manipulate it to provide various performance measures. For instance, if you divide gross profit by revenue, you arrive at a measure called *Gross Margin,* which at a glance can tell you how much of that sales figure is really translating into profits. If you divide net income by revenue, the result is a measure called

Company XYZ
Statement of Cash Flow
for the year ended December XX, 20XX

CASH FLOWS FROM OPERATING ACTIVITIES:

Net Income		15,000
Adjustments to reconcile net income to net cash provided by operating activities:		
Depreciation Expense		2,500
Increase (Decrease) in:		
Accounts Receivable	(3,000)	
Inventory	6,000	
Accounts Payable	(6,000)	
Accrued Expenses	8,000	
		5,000
Net Cash Provided by Operating Activities		22,500
CASH FLOWS FROM INVESTING ACTIVITIES:		
Purchase of Property, Equipment, Furniture		(7,500)
CASH FLOWS FROM FINANCING ACTIVITIES:		
Short-term borrowings, net	25,000	
Principal payments on Notes Payable	(10,000)	
		15,000
NET INCREASE IN CASH		30,000
CASH AT THE BEGINNING OF THE YEAR		25,000
CASH AT THE END OF THE YEAR		55,000

Figure 8-3. Company XYZ Statement of Cash Flow.

Profit Margin or *Net Margin,* considered by many an important indicator of a company's performance, one that leads to easy comparisons with the net margins of other companies.

A third financial report filed by publicly held companies is called statement of cash flows, which is designed to show the influx and outflow of cash. A typical cash flow statement, shown in Figure 8-3 (see page 140), will have these entries:

- ▣ **Net Income.** The same figure seen in the income statement.

- ▣ **Depreciation.** This is a dollar figure assigned to the declining value of such material assets as equipment. Because the equipment already has been paid for and no cash actually leaves the company for depreciation, this figure is added to the net income total.

- ▣ **Accounts Receivable and Accounts Payable.** These entries represent the change in each category from the previous period. If the totals have increased, they're added to net income. If they're in parentheses—indicating a decline—they're subtracted from net income.

- ▣ **Inventory.** The change in the value of inventory is added to or subtracted from net income, depending on whether it reflects growth or a decrease.

- ▣ **Accrued Expenses.** As with accounts receivable, accounts payable, and inventory, this figure represents a change that's added to or deducted from net income, as appropriate.

- ▣ **Net Cash Provided by Operating Activities.** We arrive at this figure by adding all the categories above.

▣ **Cash Flows From Investing Activities.** Beyond operations, we need to consider such typical business functions as investing and financing. Purchasing property, equipment, and furniture requires cash, so this figure is subtracted from net cash provided by operating activities.

▣ **Cash Flows From Financing Activities.** This is a mixed bag. Payments on debts take cash out of the flow and so are deducted from net cash provided by operating activities. However, if the firm borrows money, that figure is added to net cash provided by operating activities.

▣ **Net Cash.** We start with net income. We add in depreciation and money borrowed. We back out investments and debt service. We add or subtract the changes in accounts receivable, accounts payable, inventory, and accrued expenses, as appropriate. The result is net cash, alternatively called *cash at the end of the year.*

The statement of cash flow measures different areas of performance than the income statement and the balance sheet do. Cash flow numbers can help you detect slow-moving inventory or an inefficient accounts receivable process, to cite only several examples, more precisely than the other reports.

With these three documents in hand, you're prepared to evaluate any publicly held company in the United States as a target for investment. (For foreign-based businesses, the reporting rules may vary considerably. You may not be able to count on these three benchmark documents, at least in these forms or on a quarterly schedule.) This does not mean that you should abandon a conceptual approach to stock market investing. We've heard of investors who prospered simply by buying the shares of companies whose products they personally sampled and liked.

Product knowledge remains vital, as does some familiarity with what's happening in the sectors of each of your prospective investments. It's best to go beyond these documents to read more generally about the companies you're studying. You'll want to review the messages companies provide in their annual reports and other documents to explain and amplify the figures in their fundamental filings. They might put their own spin on things, but if you've studied the documents, you'll become your own Spinmeister, able to interpret the data without any slant from the company.

Study these documents thoroughly. Ask questions such as: Has the debt burden changed? Has accounts receivable skyrocketed? Have their been significant changes in inventory? Has the cash position improved or worsened? With several years of data typically reported, you'll be able to analyze a company's performance over time in addition to comparing its results to those of other companies.

As you do this, you'll discover that there's no magic in financial statements, no single performance measure that will tell you everything you need to know. In fact, some measures that initially appear as red flags actually can be encouraging signals. Think about your personal finances. If you buy a new car, your cash reserves decrease. If you finance your car, you may increase your long-term liabilities thanks to the interest payments.

On the other hand, your new vehicle may be more fuel-efficient and require fewer repairs than your old junker, helping you reduce operating expenses. So is your new car a wise purchase? It depends on your perspective. Corporate performance is the same way.

Consider a pharmaceutical company that slashes its R&D expenses, helping produce higher net income, net margin, and earnings per share this year. If you look at these categories in isolation, you might applaud the move as efficient cost-cutting.

But for the long term, will their reduced R&D function produce enough new products to keep them competitive? If you don't look at the company's action over both the short term and the long term, you may arrive at a distorted conclusion.

Or consider a firm that purchases a business, acquiring the new company's long-term debt as part of the purchase package. Soaring long-term debt is bad, right? Indeed, whenever one publicly held company purchases another, the stock of the acquiring company temporarily dips, reflecting shareholder concerns with the added costs. But if the new unit allows the firm to expand its product lines and increase profits—income that actually allows debt to be retired over a quicker schedule than planned before the acquisition—then the purchase is a plus for the long term.

Your review of financial data must be quantitative—knowing the numbers—as well as qualitative—knowing how the numbers relate to each other and what exactly they mean. Research is an odd business, where performance data can be illuminating and misleading at the same time.

Scoring:

> Score 4 points for d), 0 for any other answer. Many companies offer revenue and profit projections as helpful tools for their shareholders and financiers, but there's no requirement for these.

Question 3—

Which of these is not a widely used ratio that helps investors and analysts evaluate and compare stocks?

a) Acid Test Ratio.

b) AM/FM Ratio.

c) Debt/Equity Ratio.

d) Price/Earnings Ratio.

Balance sheets, income statements, and cash flow statements give you fundamental data about company performance. As we've seen, you can go beyond the data as reported to develop measures that are more sophisticated and, some would say, more revealing. We did this in Question 2 to come up with gross margins and net margins. Another series of second-level measures goes by the name of "ratios" because they indicate one performance level relative to another.

In general, ratios are designed to measure company valuation, debt-paying ability, and liquidity. Here are some of the most widely used ratios in each of the three categories:

Valuation Ratios

◼ **Price/Earnings Ratio.** More commonly known as the P/E ratio, this figure is obtained by dividing the current stock price by per-share earnings. (You won't necessarily find the share price in any of the required reports, but it's widely available.) P/E ratios can be sector-related. Growth stocks, for example, typically sell at high multiples because of the rapid growth anticipated for them. Established, old-line companies typically have lower P/E ratios because no one expects a growth spurt for them.

Also, interest rates and P/E ratios have an inverse relationship. In an environment of low interest rates, P/E ratios often increase across the board. When interest rates rise, P/E ratios tend to dip.

◼ **Book Value.** Not a ratio as such, book value is calculated by subtracting total liabilities from total assets, measures available to you on balance sheets. Sometimes called *Equity* or *Shareholders' Equity,* book value is the approximate liquidation value of a corporation.

Debt-Paying Ability Ratios

◼ **Debt Ratio.** To arrive at this ratio, divide total liabilities by total assets—same numbers that figured in book value but with a different manipulation. Debt ratios give you some sense of the indebtedness of companies relative to their assets. Generally, the lower the ratio, the better, as a heavy debt ratio can foreshadow insolvency down the road. But even this is a two-edged sword, as companies with low-debt ratios may not have borrowed enough to finance their own success.

◼ **Debt/Equity Ratio.** Dividing total liabilities by shareholders' equity—see *Book Value*—gives us the debt/equity ratio. It's another way of looking at long-term debt relative to assets.

Liquidity Ratios

◼ **Working Capital.** Current assets minus current liabilities gives you working capital, not a pure ratio but a useful measure nonetheless. Just as the debt ratio and debt/equity ratio provide a glimpse at long-term solvency, working capital is an indication of short-term liquidity that will enable the corporation to meet today's operational objectives. Working capital usually is relative to company size, so significant hiring or downsizing can affect this measure.

- ▣ **Acid Test or Quick Ratio.** A two-step calculation here. First, subtract inventory from current assets. When you get the result, divide it by liabilities. This ratio measures a corporation's immediate liquidity. Inventory is backed out of the equation because it's difficult to value and may not be so easily converted to cash.

These are among the most useful ratios, but our list is by no means exhaustive. Once you have data from the three foundation reports, you can twist and twirl them in any number of ways, if you think the result will tell you something significant about the corporations involved.

As with fundamental data, ratios have little meaning in isolation. Consider the P/E ratio, perhaps the most widely used of all ratios. If a company's stock boasts a high P/E figure, that means it's been hot with investors, popularity that might be attractive to you. But it also may mean that the share price is inflated well above any reasonable valuation; adverse impact from macroeconomic forces could force a retreat to a more realistic share price.

Does that mean a low P/E ratio is preferable? Not necessarily. A low ratio might mean that there's some quick upside potential to the stock. But it also could mean that investors have examined the fundamental characteristics of the company and found them wanting. An attractive P/E ratio won't mean a thing if the company isn't positioned for success.

Amass all the figures. Compute all the ratios. Compare information for your target company to that of similarly positioned firms—and to the company's own performance over the past several years. It's this thorough research and evaluation that will bring you success over the long term.

Scoring:

Score 4 points for b). If you answered anything else, subtract 1 point. AM/FM Ratio—are you kidding me?

Question 4—

Which of these factors should you not consider before selecting a mutual fund or funds?

a) The stocks or bonds held by the mutual fund.

b) The track record of the funds' managers.

c) The volume of publicity the funds are generating.

d) The standard deviation of each fund.

Mutual funds have become popular investments for a variety of reasons. For one thing, since they typically hold a broad selection of securities (which can include any asset class), they can appear to provide instant diversification for your portfolio, presenting far less risk than investing in a single stock or bond.

For another, investing with a group can be psychologically comforting—even though you don't necessarily know the identities of your fellow investors. Popular funds may attract hundreds or thousands of investors, including large institutional players. If they're in the boat with you, you may worry less about killer waves.

Finally, mutual funds generally provide a great deal of flexibility. You can enter or exit with ease, in sharp contrast to buying individual bonds that can lock up your money for years or even decades.

For all that, mutual funds can be an investment challenge, if only for their sheer number. Currently, there are more than 15,000 mutual funds; no two are exactly alike. Just as you spend time evaluating individual issues, you must commit to researching mutual funds.

First, consider the stocks or bonds within their investment baskets, information that's available to you through fund reports. Some funds target particular domestic sectors; technology, healthcare, and old-line industrials would be examples. Others specialize in the stocks of foreign-based companies. Still others may select from a variety of sectors, while some bill themselves as "hedge funds," protecting their investments through long and short positions. Make sure the target or specialty of any mutual fund you're considering matches your investment preferences.

You'll also want to check out the track record and investment tendencies of the manager or management team. Some observers believe that mutual funds are pure reflections of their managers. While this may be an overstatement, it's still quite true that the manager may be the single most important factor in the performance of any fund.

Study the performance history of fund managers—in their current positions and in any previous management roles. How have funds fared under their stewardship? Is there any discernible bias to their buy/sell decisions? Do they tend to retain their holdings for lengthy periods, or are they more prone to quick turnover? Getting familiar with fund managers is a must in successful selection.

If you're considering investments in multiple funds—a popular tool for diversifying—make sure you apply the same mathematical measures to your target funds as you do to individual stocks. Remember our discussion about standard deviation, a mathematical expression of risk? The risk of mutual funds can vary across a broad range, so it's useful to determine their standard deviations. With mutual funds as with individual stocks, high standard deviations mean greater risk.

Compare your funds as well by determining correlation coefficients. Even though funds typically hold many stocks or bonds, they may be investing in similar sectors and thus may correlate strongly with each other. A pair of mutual funds may rise or fall in tandem, not the scenario a diversified portfolio demands. Look for weakly or inversely correlated funds to mitigate the risk factor.

The one fund characteristic you must not heed is media hype. As we've noted before, media tend to focus on investments that are momentarily hot or disastrous. Funds may jump on the bandwagon by advertising an outstanding year. When a fund boasts of a 25 percent return this year, that tells you little about performance over the past five or 10 years. It also says nothing about the basket of stocks or bonds you may be buying into, or about the tenure of the fund manager. If the manager leaves after that huge year, the fund may be poorly positioned to repeat it.

If you find yourself attracted to a mutual fund by media hoopla or glowing word of mouth, you should interpret that as a signal to research, not buy.

Scoring:

Score 4 points for c), 0 for any other answer.

Question 5—

Which of these is not a statistical measure used to evaluate and compare mutual funds?

a) R-Squared.

b) Alpha.

c) Beta.

d) Zeta.

In studying mutual funds, you can go well beyond standard deviations and correlation coefficients—important though they be—and deploy a much broader range of statistical measures. Some of these may seem obscure, but none of them is without value. Even if you don't have access to these measures, your financial professional will. When you mull them over, remember our First Law of Statistical Measures—No Single Figure Tells All. (If Murphy can have laws, why can't we?) Study as many measures as you can to get a comprehensive view of your target funds.

Here are some of the measures, as defined by Morningstar Mutual Funds, that are most commonly used and cited:

- ▣ **Turnover Ratio.** This figure, publicly reported and required of mutual funds by the Securities and Exchange Commission, is a representation of each fund's trading activity. Funds calculate this ratio by dividing their purchases or sales, whichever is less, by their average monthly assets. Low turnover ratios often indicate a strategy geared to the long term. High figures, more than 100 percent, say, may reflect a market-timing approach and should be a caution signal to you. In addition, high turnover tends to generate more brokers' fees, expenses that fund participants must bear. If you encounter a high turnover ratio, dig into it and find out what it means.

- ▣ **Beta.** Beta expresses a fund's sensitivity to market movements by measuring the relationship between a fund's excess return over T-bills and the excess return of the benchmark index for all funds with a similar make-up. The beta of the benchmark index always is defined as 1.00. If a fund scores a beta of 0.80, for example, it's expected to perform 20 percent worse than the index when the market is up, 20 percent better than the index when the market is down.

◙ **Alpha.** Beta plays a role in alpha as well, if that's not too bizarre. Alpha measures the difference between actual and expected performance, given a fund's level of risk as suggested by beta. A positive alpha means a fund has outperformed the expectations projected by beta. A negative alpha means the reverse. (If all this alpha-beta stuff sounds like Greek to you, stick with it. The more experience you get as an investor, the more routine and meaningful these measures will become.)

◙ **R-Squared.** As beta and alpha, R-squared is a measure of risk. It reflects the percentage of a fund's movements that can be explained by the ups and downs in its benchmark index. If the R-squared value is 100, this suggests a near perfect correlation. An R-squared value of 25 indicates that only 25 percent of the fund's movements can be explained by movements in the benchmark index. Knowing R-squared values can lead you to funds with weak or inverse correlations, helping you diversify. These values also can explain why your funds are outperforming or underperforming other funds that appear to be similar.

◙ **Sharpe Ratio.** This measure entails a two-step calculation. In the first step, the 12-month return of three-month Treasury bills is subtracted from the target fund's 12-month return; that gives you the fund's excess return over that of T-bills, which are considered risk-free. In Step 2, the number reached in Step 1 is divided by the fund's standard deviation. The higher the ratio, the stronger the fund's risk-adjusted return over time. The Sharpe Ratio was developed by, and named for, Nobel Laureate William Sharpe.

Scoring:

Zeta is not a measure of anything related to mutual funds, so score 4 points for d), 0 for any other answer.

	Scoring for Chapter 8	
	Highest Possible Score	**Your Score**
Question 1	4	_____
Question 2	4	_____
Question 3	4	_____
Question 4	4	_____
Question 5	4	_____
CHAPTER TOTALS	20	_____

9 Getting Up Close and Personal With Risk

When people shy away from the stock market, it's most often because they're frightened of the risks involved with an institution they may not understand very well. Everyone knows bank accounts. Everyone knows certificates of deposit. Choosing these cash assets as vehicles for investment appears to be safe. The irony, of course, is that cash assets aren't safe at all. They have baggage—inflation risk, which can reduce the buying power of the principal, even though its dollar value may remain the same or grow slightly.

Thus, it's clear that successful investing involves getting up close and personal with risk, understanding this hydra-headed monster in all its guises, and developing an investment strategy that falls within your risk tolerance zone. All investing involves a fundamental trade-off—the prospect of gain swapped for a certain level of risk. If you know the risks associated with each asset class, you'll also understand the trade-offs and be better prepared to evaluate them. That, in turn, will help you create a sound investment plan.

Investors who shun the stock market seem to be saying:

"I'm staying out because I might lose money, which would force me to work harder, save even more money, and perhaps abandon my financial goals."

Here's what they should be saying:

"Because of inflation and the desire to meet my financial goals in the most prudent and productive way possible, I must develop a diversified investment plan that includes stocks. I realize that the value of my investment in securities will fluctuate, but over the long term, I'll be more successful than if I didn't invest in stocks at all."

If that's too big a mouthful to serve as your personal mantra, let's make it more concrete with an example of the hidden risks of supposedly safe investments. Couple A implements a conservative, risk-averse investment plan. Their excess money goes into "safe" vehicles, such as bank accounts and CDs, which give them an average annual return of 5 percent. (They likely wouldn't earn that much at today's rates, but let's give these timid souls the benefit of the doubt.) If Couple A invests $200 each month, after 20 years, their total investment of $48,000 will grow to approximately $83,100.

Now, contrast that scenario with that of Couple B, who map out a more aggressive investment program that features both greater risk—in the form of stocks—and an average annual return of 10 percent. Over 20 years, their investment of $48,000 will grow to approximately $154,600—$71,500 more than Couple A's nest egg. The same amount of money was invested, but it was invested more productively.

Think of what that extra $71,500 means. Couple B will have an easier time financing their children's college education. They can retire earlier if they choose, travel more if they choose. And they can relax, because they know they have enough in reserve to cover any circumstance that may arise. Sure, Couple B took on risk by investing in the market, but it was a trade-off they understood and accepted. And Couple A's strategy, though nominally safer, was hardly without risk. If inflation averages 4 percent over their 20 years of savings, their growth will barely outpace inflation, leaving them not much better off than they were in terms of purchasing power.

Risk, in short, *must* be understood and *can* be managed. Our next series of questions probes your understanding of risk...and should help you become a competent risk manager.

Question 1—

The best definition for "market risk" is:

a) The risk that you'll lose your entire principal in the market.

b) The risk that the value of your investment will fluctuate, based on the overall economy and market conditions.

c) The risk that you won't have ready access to your money.

d) The risk that the next time you talk to your broker, he'll be phoning you collect from Tahiti.

Market risk is what investors most fear, although it is subject to misinterpretation. Of course there's a chance that you'll lose your entire principal. This happens so infrequently, though, that those who analyze the market regularly have refined the concept of market risk to make it more useful. They think of it as *principal fluctuation*. In this more advanced definition, the key concern is not loss of the entire principal but the degree of fluctuation your investment will experience on a day-to-day basis.

The price fluctuations at the heart of market risk are a product of the overall economy and market conditions—macro forces, if you will—not the performance of any one company in which you may have invested. Sluggish consumer spending, poor performance of the market in general, and disappointing showing by a particular sector are all market risks that can affect any of the stocks in your portfolio.

Strange as it may seem, even upside market momentum can create risk. We witnessed this in the late 1990s when some investors assumed that the stock of any dotcom would skyrocket. When the bubble ultimately burst, even fundamentally sound companies and their investors suffered the consequences.

But the macro forces that help make market risk more than a hypothetical concept usually are negative. The terrorist attacks of 9/11 and the accounting scandals of Enron, WorldCom, and others are but a few recent examples. Each eroded investor confidence and each sent the market into a tailspin that affected you—no matter which stocks were in your portfolio. That's market risk come home to roost. Each market slide is followed by a recovery, but no one can predict the precise timing of the recovery—yet another reason why a market-timing approach is fraught with peril. Sometimes the market recovers before earnings actually improve, rallying in anticipation of a rebound that's still down the road. Other times, investors hunker down and wait for signs of recovery before jumping back in. This mass reluctance delays the very recovery the pack is waiting for.

How do you cope with market risk short of staying out of stocks completely? You remember that you're investing for the long term. Your degree of market risk is directly related to the holding period of your investment. If you bail out of the market when it slumps, you're hurt. If you stick with it, you're hurt by the slump but healed by the subsequent recovery.

We know that, over any 15- to 17-year period in the past, the S&P 500 has provided only positive returns; investors who maintained their market presence throughout any of those periods made money. It always must be noted that past performance is no guarantee of future results. If your time horizon is a minimum of 15 years, investing in S&P 500–comparable stocks or funds brings very little market risk. Sounds easy, yet many long-time investors are transformed to short-term market-timers the very first time their portfolios take a hit. This is just the sort of emotional response that makes market risk a market reality.

Stick with the plan. Build a diversified portfolio and stay the course. Market fluctuation is an unavoidable aspect of the investing experience. Take comfort in the knowledge that, even though current dislocations seem particularly devastating to us, the market has been rocked by similar disasters in the past and always has rebounded. Some sectors are harder hit than others; this, too, is a historic feature of down markets. In our own times, travel and entertainment companies may have suffered the most in the aftermath of the 9/11 attacks. Yet they bounced back. A diversified portfolio will likely provide you with enough winners to offset the performance in temporarily troubled sectors.

Volatility is a characteristic of the market that's unlikely to change. Before investing in stocks, you'll need to determine your tolerance for significant market swings. If market risk keeps you out of stocks, you almost certainly won't be as productive with your money, and your overall goals could be jeopardized. (See the previous hapless Couple A.) Buying and selling may be challenging aspects of investing, but the most difficult task of all may be staying put...and staring down market risk.

Scoring:

Score 4 points for b). If you answered d), give yourself 1 point. As we say, a sense of humor in investing can help you maintain perspective and avoid emotional decisions.

Question 2—

The best definition for "credit risk" is:

a) The chance that you won't be able to get credit because of poorly performing investments.

b) The risk that your credit card issuers will demand immediate payment.

c) The volatility associated with individual stocks or bonds as it relates to the financial stability of the issuing companies.

d) All of the above.

Market risk involves the dangers to your portfolio from market movements generated by macroeconomic forces. Credit risk is the threat provided by the potentially uneven performance of individual companies in which you might invest due to their financial instability or changes in their financial stability. Businesses that aren't making money or are carrying significant debt on their balance sheets often present a high degree of credit risk; their performance in the market is likely to be volatile.

Oddly enough, some investors actually seek out companies that pose significant credit risk in the belief that the greater the risk, the greater the potential return. Buy the stock of an obscure, no-profit start-up, this theory goes, and you'll be in on the ground floor when the company takes off. This type of speculative investing in technology and Internet stocks was the rage in the late 1990s. Investors in dubious dotcoms soon learned that they weren't on the ground floor at all; they had many more levels to fall. In the stock market, it may be true that great risk precedes great reward, but it doesn't follow that great risk *always* leads to great reward.

While credit risk is primarily a characteristic of stocks, it also is a feature of individual municipal and corporate bonds. Fixed-income assets may be less risky than stocks, but they're not without dangers. When California's Orange County defaulted on its municipal bonds in the 1990s, it persuasively demonstrated the perils of credit risk in the fixed-income asset class. With bonds, the relationship between risk and reward is clear and direct. The higher the interest rates, the lower the quality of the bond and the greater the corresponding risk.

They may express different types of danger, but market risk and credit risk can be a deadly duo. The macro economic forces that cause market risk will exert an impact on all portfolios; the extent to which your portfolio suffers is determined by the credit risk of the individual assets in your portfolio. A certain degree of credit risk is unavoidable, but you can limit it by studying the financial statements we reviewed in Chapter 8 to ensure that you pick strong and stable companies for your portfolio. In addition, ask these questions about each prospective investment:

- ◼ How would an economic slowdown or recession affect the financial stability of this company?

- ◼ Would terrorist attacks or other disruptive political events have an inordinate impact on this company?

- ◼ How competitive is the sector within which this business operates, and will increasing competition tend to reduce the company's market share?

To evaluate credit risk, you'll need to know the numbers— and go beyond them to the qualitative questions that assess the financial stability of target companies in today's market and less certain world of the future. Through your research, you may find that adjustments to your current holdings are in order.

For example, by studying past performance, you may determine that each stock in your portfolio responds negatively (credit risk) to a rise in interest rates (market risk). If you sell some of those issues and replace them with stocks that respond well to rising interest rates, you'll achieve diversification on this front and reduce both market risk and credit risk. That's what you can do when you understand market risk, credit risk, and the interplay between them.

Scoring:

Score 4 points for c), 0 for any other answer.

Question 3—

Interest rate risk has the biggest potential impact on which asset class?

a) Cash assets.

b) Fixed-income assets.

c) Equity assets.

d) Real estate assets.

In their quest for a guaranteed return, risk-adverse investors often settle on fixed-income assets, believing that this will insulate them from the ups and downs of macroeconomic forces and the uncertainties of individual stocks. While they may escape the brunt of market risk and credit risk, they find themselves at the mercy of still another danger—interest rate risk.

Interest rate risk may be thought of as a comparative risk, that is, it's a risk that becomes real when your fixed return pales before the returns available in other asset classes—primarily stocks—due to changing economic conditions. Your fixed-return assets lock you into a relatively low return when there are much better investments available.

Here's a concrete example of interest rate risk at work. In the late 1980s and early 1990s, investors in certificates of deposit were on top of the world, enjoying annual interest rates of 8 percent to 10 percent. Many CD holders were able to finance retirement from their interest gains alone. Then the economy turned upside down, and CD interest rates dropped dramatically, to 2 percent or lower in some cases. Those new retirees found themselves with an unappetizing set of choices. They could research other, more aggressive investments—and it was pretty late in the day for that—or they could swallow hard and accept a reduced standard of living.

Of course, CD investors could have shifted their funds to other asset classes when their CDs matured, but focusing on fixed-income assets seems to involve something akin to psychological fixation. We saw that in the early 2000s. Interest rates continued their decline, but this time, the stock market also plunged, providing cheaper prices and a much more appealing entry point. Sounds like an easy decision—shift a large chunk of your money into the stock market. Yet many investors clung tenaciously to fixed-income assets and their suddenly meager returns.

Because stock prices had declined so dramatically, a great many investors were afraid to transfer their money from seemingly safe fixed-income vehicles to the stock market, even if they were earning a paltry 2 percent with their CDs. In this situation, even a modest market recovery would enable investors to realize improved returns over fixed-income vehicles. Conservative investors, however, can't tolerate the uncertain timing of market recoveries, so they usually opt for fixed-income assets and the perils of interest rate risk.

The fact of the matter is that swings in interest rates can be as unpredictable as changes in the stock market, and CDs aren't the only investment vehicle affected by moody interest rates. Bonds and bond mutual funds, to cite another example, can be directly and adversely influenced by changes in interest rates. When interest rates rise, bond valuations decline. The reverse also is true. Decreasing interest rates bring increasing bond valuations.

Imagine that you own a bond paying 6 percent, only to find that soaring interest rates increase the payout rate of newly issued bonds to 7 percent. If you try to sell your 6 percent bond, you'll be forced to reduce your price. If you don't, investors will spurn your offer and purchase newly issued bonds at the more attractive 7 percent payout rate. That's the way interest rate risk *can* affect bondholders.

Moreover, since the Federal Reserve uses interest rate changes to control the pace of economic growth, such modifications are inevitable. So it's important to understand the condition of the economy and what direction interest rates may be moving before settling into fixed-income investments. If interest rates are historically high and likely to decline, then it may be time to select long-term fixed-income assets, if that's your class of choice. But if interest rates are historically low and poised to rise, investment vehicles with shorter maturities may be in order.

Some investors in fixed-income assets make the classic mistake of chasing performance—a faux pas more commonly associated with equity assets. When the stock market drops, they chase the seemingly more secure environment of fixed-income assets, paying no heed to the cyclical nature of interest rates. The pattern repeats itself over and over—interest rates decline to a point where the economy is stimulated; the Fed hikes interest rates to keep the economy from overheating; the economy cools off, interest rates decline, and the pattern repeats yet again.

If you understand the cycles, you can position your investments to take advantage of the up cycles and avoid the dangers of the *down* cycles, rather than chase performance. If the stock market has achieved negative returns and interest rates have fallen, some investors scurry to the safe harbor of a CD, tying up their money for as long as five years for a negligible return, only to kick themselves a year later when interest rates increase.

Economists have developed a tool called the *yield curve* to help us make the connection between interest rates and bond maturities. The yield curve plots the relationship between yields to maturity (the vertical axis) and time to maturity (the horizontal axis) for bonds with similar characteristics. A good place to review and study yield curves is BondsOnline, *www.bondsonline.com*

Figure 9-1 shows a yield curve with a "normal" pattern. The upward slope of the curve indicates that interest rates rise as maturity periods lengthen. When this scenario prevails, you'll earn more on a 5-year bond than on a 1-year-bond. The yield curve usually maintains a normal slope when the economy is moving along consistently and no Fed intervention is anticipated.

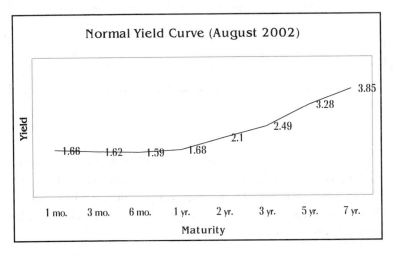

Figure 9-1.

When the yield curve slopes downward, as it does in Figure 9-2, it indicates an inverse relationship between maturities and interest rates—the longer the maturity, the lower the interest rate. We get this pattern when interest rates have peaked, the economy is likely to turn sluggish, and the Fed may act to lower interest rates. Inverted yield curves have been a consistently accurate predictor of economic slowdowns.

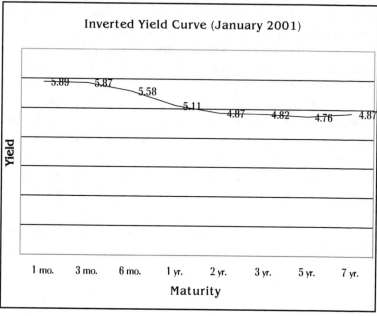

Figure 9-2.

If you follow the yield curve, you can minimize your interest rate risk in bonds. When the curve is inverted, it may lead you to select a short-term bond at today's interest rates, rather than invest in a long-term vehicle that you project will provide lower interest rates at maturity.

Scoring:

Since fixed-income assets are most vulnerable to interest rate risk, score 4 points for b). Give yourself 1 point for any other answer because interest rate fluctuation has the potential to affect all asset classes.

Question 4—

The asset class most susceptible to inflation risk is:

a) Cash assets.

b) Fixed-income assets.

c) Equity assets.

d) Real estate assets.

Market risk and credit risk, of course, are perils associated with aggressive investing that usually involves equity assets. Interest rate risk primarily affects fixed-income assets. But there also are dangers related to the passive savings that are characteristic of cash assets. Among them is inflation. It's one of the most important factors that you must understand when establishing your financial goals and game plan.

Simply put, inflation represents the decline in purchasing power of your money. Because of inflation, $100 that you spend today will not buy the same amount of goods and services five years from now. If you do the grocery shopping for your family, you know the meaning of inflation very well. You're spending much more for the same amount of food than you did even a few years ago. That's the power of inflation.

Apply this same lesson to your investing and you'll get an alarming sense of the risk of inflation. Let's suppose that your income need today is $40,000 per year, and that you want to retire in 25 years. If we assume an average annual inflation rate of 4.8 percent—the actual average over the past 25 years—your annual income need 25 years from now would be slightly more than $129,000. And that's assuming that your needs won't change, a risky assumption at best. If you don't incorporate inflation into your financial planning, you're not likely to get where you want to go.

Here's another way to look at it. If inflation this year checks in at 5 percent, and your conservative cash investments earn 2 percent, your purchasing power has declined by 3 percent. You're not actually losing money, but you might as well be, because your purchasing power is dropping. Inflation is insidious and lethal, like the slow-acting venom of certain snakes. You don't know you've been financially paralyzed until you try to buy something.

Once inflation is loose on the scene, you can't reverse its impact on your portfolio. Prevention—a less conservative investing strategy—is the only way to stay ahead of inflation. We know that cash assets are particularly vulnerable to inflation, fixed-income assets slightly less so. In fact, once taxes are figured in, the returns from fixed-income assets underperform inflation in many years. Keeping at least part of your portfolio in equity assets is perhaps the best way to minimize the impact of inflation.

This is especially true during your retirement years. When you're working, inflation may be offset by salary increases, which often reflect the annual inflation rate. This is not so during retirement, when you have no salary. When they reach their "golden years," many investors shift their assets from equity to fixed-income vehicles, thinking that they can't handle the risks of the market at that stage in their lives. Yet this almost always precipitates the very problem it's intended to prevent—loss of portfolio purchasing power. If sound investing principles got you to a well-financed retirement, it's those sound principles that will keep you there. If you turn conservative and allow inflation a beachhead on your portfolio, the retirement lifestyle you enjoy could be a casualty.

Inflation affects all assets by decreasing the dollar value of their returns. But because of their higher potential return, equity assets can be the most effective hedge against inflation. In fact, it might not be too strong to say that if you're looking to the stock market to get rich, you've come for the wrong reason. But if you select the stock market as a tool to neutralize inflation and maintain the purchasing power of your portfolio, you're on the right track.

Perhaps the bottom line on risk—in all four of its variants—is that *no investor can avoid it or conquer it*. But you can understand risk, and you can develop an investment strategy that's consistent with your return expectations and risk tolerance. If you appreciate and accept risk-related trade-offs, you'll chart an even course on the sea of investment, and you won't set sail through turbulent waters to chase the White Whale known as performance.

Scoring:

Since cash assets are most vulnerable to inflation, score 4 points for a). As noted, inflation has an impact on all asset classes, so give yourself 1 point for any other answer.

	Scoring for Chapter 9	
	Highest Possible Score	**Your Score**
Question 1	4	_____
Question 2	4	_____
Question 3	4	_____
Question 4	4	_____
CHAPTER TOTALS	16	_____

10 Monitoring and Adjusting—The Unsung Heroes of Successful Investing

C hange is just about the only thing certain in investing. Even if you have created the best possible portfolio for your objectives—you're riding high along the Efficient Frontier—something is sure to happen that affects the productivity of your investments. If you don't regularly monitor your portfolio and implement the appropriate responses to new economic conditions, your ability to achieve your goals may be threatened.

Change is inevitable; your commitment to respond to change must be equally constant. Your adjustments will vary across a wide range. At times, you may need a radical shake-up in your holdings. At other times, you'll decide that standing pat makes the most sense. We can't predict what adjustments you'll make, only that they will be necessary.

Let's take a look at change in action and how it affects you. Suppose your ideal portfolio has its value allocated according to this formula: 40 percent in domestic stocks and mutual funds; 40 percent in the stocks of foreign-based companies and mutual funds targeting emerging markets; and 20 percent in fixed-income assets, such as T-bills and bonds. It's a formula that appears to be working well for you. So well, in fact, that when domestic stocks soar in a bull market, that otherwise gratifying development presents you with something of a problem.

Now, because the value of your domestic stocks has skyrocketed, 60 percent of your portfolio value is in that category, rather than the 40 percent you had allocated originally. If you're monitoring your portfolio, you'll be aware of what's happening and prepare to make adjustments. These adjustments can range from liquidating some of your domestic stock holdings and pocketing the proceeds, to selling off some domestic stocks and using the gains to purchase additional foreign issues and fixed-income assets, thereby restoring the 40-40-20 balance of your portfolio.

Another option is to do nothing. But look what happens if you stand back and admire your handiwork. Your carefully crafted asset allocation now is out of whack, and you are exposed to greater risk because of the imbalance in your holdings. You didn't create the imbalance (macroeconomic forces and the market did), but you have a higher risk profile all the same. In this situation, it should be clear that doing nothing is not a viable option—unless careful study reveals that your revised allocation, on which you've landed quite by accident, will work well in the new economic environment.

The operative words there are "careful study." Portfolio monitoring and adjustment should become part of your regular investing routine. The questions below will probe your familiarity with some of the most important aspects of monitoring and adjustment. These tasks may not bring you the high that you experience with your initial buy decisions, but they're the unsung heroes of investing.

Question 1—

When you monitor your portfolio, you should review it against which of the following:

a) Your time frame and goals.

b) The benchmark index for your portfolio.

c) Total return of your investments.

d) All of the above.

Regular review and rebalancing—the term financial professionals use for adjustments to a portfolio—are essential elements in successful investing. Circumstances change, sometimes rapidly, sometimes glacially. Your portfolio must change to match the new environment if you're to stay on track for your goals.

Understanding those goals, and your time frame for achieving them, will provide a solid foundation for your review and rebalancing. If you have short-term goals—for example, making enough from earnings to finance a new car or home—then clearly you'll be looking for the maximum return over the shortest possible time frame. If you're not getting that return early in the game, then you may need to modify your holdings in short order.

Your time frame also will affect the frequency of your portfolio review. If you need that new car within six months, annual portfolio reviews won't do you much good. You'll need to review early and often. Short-term approaches are quite risky; during a three- to six-month period, the market and your portfolio can go just about any which way. Nevertheless, if you have immediate goals, you'll need immediate reviews and corresponding adjustments.

More commonly, though, investors are in the market for the long haul. Now, as you review your portfolio, you can measure its performance against your long-term goals. Is your portfolio getting you where you want to go over time? If you ask that question, you can factor in the historical performance of the market and avoid emotional reactions to short-term aberrations.

That's where *total return* comes into play. Total return is not simply the dividend yield combined with interest earned. These are components of total return, which also includes capital appreciation or depreciation of the asset.

Consider this example, drawn from the real estate asset class. You purchase a rental property valued at $100,000, and you earn rental income of $10,000 that first year. That gives you an income yield of 10 percent. However, you sell the property one year later for $105,000, meaning that your capital appreciation is $5,000, or 5 percent. That works out to a total return of 15 percent for the year. When you focus on total return, you're better able to judge the suitability and stability of any investment. If you're income-oriented, yield matters. If you're looking for long-term growth, yield isn't nearly as important.

Zooming in on total return will also give you a clear picture of the risks involved with your investments. Generally, the higher the total return potential, the more risk your investment carries. Think about limited partnerships that invest in such properties as strip malls, office equipment, or Broadway plays. These may provide you with a high yield, but the back end of the proposition—the ultimate success of the properties—is risky. Here you have a high potential total return with significant risk.

Yet there are exceptions. A mature blue chip company may increase its distributions to shareholders rather that invest all its excess money in the expansion of the business. In this case, you have increased yield with little additional risk because the company involved is fundamentally stable. If you analyze all the components of total return, you'll have an easier time evaluating risk versus reward.

As you focus on total return, consider also the time-period–specific factors that may have influenced the performance of your portfolio. Was financial euphoria on the loose? Was the economy in the throes of recession? Did inflation rear its ugly head? Look especially at the performance of your investments when they were technically "out of favor." That will sharpen your appreciation for the downside potential and help you set realistic expectations.

Your reviews should include a comparison of your portfolio's performance with that of its benchmark index, the index with which it most closely corresponds. The idea is to use an index that gives you an apples-to-apples comparison. If your portfolio is weighted 40 percent to foreign-based companies in well-developed countries, for example, you would want to compare its performance to an index with similar weighting. When you do that, you can reasonably attribute any variances to the individual assets within your portfolio.

Comparisons between asset classes aren't always as helpful because they don't necessarily take risk into account. The performance of equity assets often outshines that of fixed-income assets, but the risks can be correspondingly greater. Interest rates on CDs are guaranteed; dividends on stocks are as unpredictable as the next board meeting, when directors may increase or slash the dividend. Thus, a side-by-side comparison of performance in these two asset classes doesn't tell you enough.

Finally, if you're investing for the long term, remember not to be swayed by disappointing short-term results. Any single year, or even a three-year period, can bring dramatic swings in the market. When Jeremy Siegel conducted a longitudinal study of the market, he looked at extremely lengthy subperiods—54 years was the shortest stretch—and noted remarkably consistent performance, ranging from 6.6 percent average return for the period between 1871 through 1925, to 7.5 percent average return for the current period beginning with World War II. That's a remarkably narrow range, suggesting that we pay little attention to the fluctuations of a given year or several-year period. During your portfolio reviews, use that performance range as your guide.

Scoring:

The best answer, worth 4 points, is d). Since all the yardsticks we've listed are important, score 1 point for any other answer.

Question 2—

Which of these is the primary goal of portfolio rebalancing?

a) To restore the original balance of the portfolio.

b) To protect against risk in the face of dynamic market conditions.

c) To "beat the market" and take advantage of changing conditions.

d) Any or all of the above, depending on your goals and style.

In his book *Asset Allocation—Balancing Financial Risk,* Roger C. Gibson identifies three principle approaches to portfolio rebalancing. The most common is known as *passive allocation*, which involves taking the steps necessary to return to the original formula.

Let's again consider our example of a portfolio that allocates 40 percent to domestic stocks and mutual funds, 40 percent to stocks of foreign-based companies and mutual funds targeting emerging markets, and 20 percent to fixed-income assets, such as T-bills and bonds. Let's further assume that a spurt in the domestic stock market knocks the original alignment out of kilter, since we now have more than 40 percent of our value in domestic stocks and funds.

An investor employing the passive allocation approach to rebalancing will do what it takes to restore that 40-40-20 allocation. That could involve selling off some of the domestic stocks, purchasing additional assets in the other categories, or both. Returning to the original allocation time after time makes sense, provided the formula remains productive. If the allocation won't work in the new environment, restoring it only will compound your problems.

In that situation, one solution is to start from scratch, re-evaluating the correlation of your assets and developing a new allocation. Be mindful, however, that asset allocation is a long-term strategy. You may judge it a failure because of disappointing current performance, but your formula still may click over the long haul. A sector represented in your portfolio may be out of favor for years before it responds positively and makes up for lost time. That's the nature of the risk/return relationship, a fundamental principle of the market.

A second approach to portfolio adjustments is what Gibson calls *dynamic asset allocation*, through which investors try to exploit changing market conditions expected to prevail for some time. When prices decline, stocks are sold to reduce the possibility of further loss. When stock prices rise, stocks are purchased so that gains from the up market can be maximized. In our example, with domestic stocks rising, our hypothetical investor using a dynamic asset allocation strategy would load up on domestic stocks to try and participate in the rally while it lasts. Notice that in this approach, little or no attention is paid to the original asset allocation, which becomes an early casualty of market momentum.

The third approach, *tactical asset allocation*, is what might be called the contrarian spin on portfolio rebalancing. In this model, investors observe a market rally or decline but assume that the direction of the market soon will be reversed and reallocate assets accordingly. In our example of the 40-40-20 allocation with domestic stocks on the rise, a tactical asset allocator will sell the stocks, believing that the rally soon will give way to an inevitable slump. This might be called the "buy low, sell high" approach, whereas dynamic allocation could be summed up as "buy high, sell low."

As with dynamic allocation, tactical allocation pays little heed to the original scheme. Nor is there much concern in these two approaches about the resulting mix, once the appropriate buying or sell-off has taken place. Whether that ends up 60-30-10 or 30-50-20 isn't really considered in these two strategies. They're based on reactions to market conditions rather than adherence to a Golden Formula.

For us, dynamic asset allocation and tactical asset allocation smack too much of market timing. The markets are remarkably true to form, despite the inevitable short-term volatility. If you doubt it, look at Figure 10-1 on page 179, which shows Dow Jones Industrial Average performance for three selected decades. Note that volatility is a constant, as are profits for those who stayed the course. Even in the first turbulent decade of the 20th century, investors who remained in the market were rewarded with average annual gains of 7.6 percent. Closer to our time, the year 1987 brought a precipitous stock market crash, yet investors who endured the slump profited on the year.

No one can predict what the market will do over the short term, so rebalancing that's based on today's trends takes you

Dow Jones Industrial Average					
Year	**Return**	**Year**	**Return**	**Year**	**Return**
1900	7.6	1950	17.6	1980	14.9
1901	-8.7	1951	14.4	1981	-9.8
1902	-.04	1952	8.4	1982	19.6
1903	-23.6	1953	-3.8	1983	20.3
1904	41.7	1954	44.0	1984	-3.7
1905	38.7	1955	20.8	1985	27.7
1906	-2.3	1956	2.3	1986	22.6
1907	-37.7	1957	-12.8	1987	2.3
1908	46.6	1958	34.0	1988	11.8
1909	15.0	1959	16.4	1989	27.0

Figure 10-1. Historical Dow Jones Data.

into uncertain territory. If you deploy dynamic asset allocation or tactical asset allocation, at the very least, calculate and
analyze your resulting allocation once you've made your adjustments. That will give you a starting point for rebalancing
in the future.

Scoring:

While we strongly favor rebalancing that takes
us back to our original formula, we must
acknowledge that experienced professionals
use any or all of these approaches. So we'll grit
our teeth and award 4 points for d), 2 points
for any other answer.

Question 3—

How often should you rebalance your portfolio?

a) At least twice a year.

b) As market conditions dictate.

c) Whenever your original asset allocation formula has been seriously distorted.

d) Any or all of the above.

As we've noted, investing in multiple asset classes and sectors, with a percentage of your portfolio assigned to each class or sector, provides you with diversification and the chance for maximum gains with minimum risk. Alas, the markets will pay little respect to your carefully crafted formula. They'll do what they will, wreaking havoc with your balance. It can happen subtly over time, or it can happen with a dramatic, immediate swing in a sector or asset class. The question here is: When should you step in to rebalance, that is, to sell some assets and purchase others, so that your original allocation is restored?

A good schedule is to review your portfolio at least *twice each year*, and to rebalance it whenever your allocation formula has taken a serious hit or economic conditions warrant. In your review, compare your original asset allocation with the current status. If you find only a slight variance, you may be satisfied with doing nothing. Review in this case doesn't imply rebalance. Given that you're investing for the long term, you may find many years when no changes are necessary.

Should you encounter significant variations from your original allocation, it's time to revisit both the soundness of the formula and current performance against that formula. If you believe that your original allocation is sound, then you'll need to consider divesting assets in the overweighted sectors or classes and using the proceeds to purchase assets in underweighted sectors or classes—all to restore your original allocation. (Don't be overly concerned with minute variations from your formula. If the figures are within, for exmple, 2 percent of your original allocation, that's probably an acceptable tolerance.)

While this sounds fairly straightforward, many investors recoil at the notion of selling some assets with outstanding recent performance and purchasing laggards. This may seem contrary to common sense, and yet investors in technology stocks a few years back probably wish they had displayed a little more uncommon sense by selling some of their tech issues and reinvesting the proceeds in less volatile asset classes or sectors. It's very easy for last year's winners to become this year's losers. Remember, you created an allocation formula in part to minimize your risk. If you continue to believe in your formula, stick with it and restore it, no matter how hot or cold any one sector or asset class may appear.

Significant market changes—both current and anticipated—also can trigger portfolio modifications. Obvious events to consider would be changes in the management of any mutual funds in which you've invested. If a new manager introduces a philosophy of frequent asset turnover, for example, that may cause you to rethink your position in that fund.

A prospective shift in interest rates—the yield curve in Chapter 9 should help you here—also could move you to reposition some of your money. These actions aren't portfolio rebalancing in the classic sense. Rather, they're preemptive strikes that can prevent or limit damage to your asset allocation.

While semi-annual portfolio reviews and rebalancing as needed strike us as a reasonable schedule, some managers of large funds go well beyond that. They automatically rebalance their portfolios on a quarterly or even monthly basis, always restoring the mix to the original allocation. If you're managing your portfolio yourself, this approach might be rather time-consuming. But it does eliminate any temptation to succumb to market timing. That's always a plus.

Scoring:

> The best answer is d), since any of the other answers could serve as the impetus for portfolio rebalancing. Score 4 points for d). However, since none of the answers is incorrect, give yourself 2 points for a), b), or c).

Question 4—

As you consider the rebalancing of your portfolio, newspaper and analysts' ratings of stocks and bonds should:

a) Guide all your decisions.

b) Be a factor in your decisions.

c) Inspire you to research their top picks.

d) Be used to wrap any leftover fish.

Newspapers and analysts are at once bane and blessing to investors. They can alert us to developments that otherwise might slip by unnoticed; they can ask probing questions of CEOs and CFOs to unearth truth that otherwise might go unreported. Yet the information they provide, particularly in the area of rankings, can be superficial, misleading, or both, and therefore must be treated with extreme caution.

Ranking systems are an absolute hodgepodge. Some newspapers and financial newsletters award stars; the more stars, the better. A four-star fund has performed better than a two-star fund, for example. Others use a numerical or lettering system, but even here there's little standardization. In some systems, a ranking of 1 may indicate the top-performing group, 5 indicates the stocks or funds with poorest performance. Yet others reverse that, giving the highest numbers to the best performers. This can make for some tricky comparisons between ratings systems.

Even beyond this chaos, there's little uniformity in what data are being measured. In some cases, rankings are based on year-to-date performance. In other cases, ratings reflect performance for the past year—including part of the last calendar year. Ratings may also reflect pre-tax return, which may mean little to you in your particular tax situation.

If you can make sense of this hash and figure out what's being measured for which period, there's still the matter of whether performance over the relatively short period of one year is enough to trigger repositioning of your assets. The ratings may tell you, once you sort them all out, what a stock or fund did over a particular year, but they don't tell you why. Market volatility may have been responsible for weakness in a particular sector or asset class in a given year; that same volatility could transform that sector or asset into a superstar the next year.

Understanding the environment in which the market has been operating will help you put rankings in the proper context. If you slavishly follow the ratings and swap all your two-star funds for four-star vehicles, you're letting the rankings seduce you into chasing performance.

Because they're omnipresent, rankings are just about impossible to avoid entirely. If you do peruse them, favor those that provide calendar-year data. We tend to view the market environment in calendar-year increments, so rankings based on year-to-date performance provide better entree to overall market review.

Perhaps the best way to view ratings is as a trigger for research. If a high ranking of a fund excites you, if a low ranking worries you, spend some time researching those assets. You'll be better prepared to make the right decisions than those who treat analysts as latter-day gods.

Our discussion about the impact of media and analysts wouldn't be complete if we didn't mention potential conflicts of interest on the part of those providing unsolicited advice. We would be the last people to engage in media-bashing; reporters and analysts provide valuable, at times irreplaceable, information for investors.

But from time to time, the nasty little conflict of interest problem bubbles up to the surface: A reporter for a prestigious newspaper is busted for profiting on insider information. A major financial services firm gets caught touting companies for which it was underwriting initial public offerings. It doesn't take too many such scandals to inspire tough questions about the credibility of all financial journalists and analysts. Are newspapers printing flattering feature stories on the XYZ Fund because the XYZ Fund advertises heavily in those newspapers? Are analysts recommending certain stocks because they own shares in those stocks?

Unless publishers, reporters, and analysts implement full disclosure of their assets—revelation we don't anticipate anytime soon—we simply can't be sure of any conflicts of interest. Perhaps it's best to approach media and analysts' reports with neither blind faith nor rock-hard skepticism, but a little of each wouldn't hurt.

Scoring:

> Score 4 points for c). If you answered d), you get 1 point. We're 10 chapters in and your wit remains intact.

	Scoring for Chapter 10	
	Highest Possible Score	**Your Score**
Question 1	4	_____
Question 2	4	_____
Question 3	4	_____
Question 4	4	_____
CHAPTER TOTALS	16	_____

11 Taxes— Make Them Part of Your Investment Planning

Taxes play a role in most financial matters, yet sadly, most people fail to consider their taxes until those few harried weeks before the returns are due. Many people would be hard-pressed to tell you their current tax brackets, let alone discuss the tax implications of their investments. Yet gaining an understanding of how your investments affect your taxes is a must if you want to plan the most tax-efficient program and achieve your most important goals.

Perhaps the most vital concept to grasp in this key area is that "after-tax" returns are what count. It does you little good to realize substantial gains in your portfolio if your profits are gobbled up by taxes. Think of this sequence: after-tax return, after-tax income, after-tax estate. That's the tax planning drill you want to go through with each prospective investment. What's the likely after-tax return? How will that affect my after-tax income? What will be my resulting after-tax estate?

We tend to regard our after-tax income as our paychecks— what's left after our employers take out all those deductions noted on the stubs. Yet this can be a misleading indication of useable income because so many other categories come into play. Tax deductions, tax exemptions, investment proceeds, mortgage interest, out-of-pocket medical expenses can all affect after-tax income, and may have nothing to do with your salary.

Each investment you make has potential tax consequences. Some investments produce dividends. Some generate interest. Still others appreciate and result in capital gains. Some investments will provide all these benefits in a given year—a red-letter day for you, but one with tax consequences. Changes within your portfolio can have tax ramifications as well.

Estate taxes are still another matter for consideration. While federal estate taxes are being phased out, Congress may resurrect them at any time. And the federal phase-out has done nothing to moderate any state or local inheritance taxes. Moreover, certain types of taxes can follow you to the grave. Consider the example of a 401(k) plan, which has been growing on a tax-deferred basis. If you pass on before taking distributions and paying taxes on them, your heirs will be subject to taxes on all the money in the account.

It's clear that before you can implement a tax plan to preserve as much of your wealth as possible for you and your heirs, you must first understand your tax situation, then get a grasp on the tax consequences of each investment you're considering. The next series of questions will probe your familiarity with these issues.

If you discover you're not too familiar with them, don't be disheartened. Professional advice on taxes is quite accessible. Even people who consider themselves world-class investors may have tax advisors—the discipline is simply too complicated and changeable to grasp without counsel. The year 2001, to cite just one example, brought more than 400 changes to U.S. tax law. Accountants take professional education courses to keep up, so it makes sense to tap their wisdom.

Important as they are, taxes never should be the primary factor in your investment decisions. You're still looking for the best long-term value in your asset selection; taxes are *one* factor to be considered in a much broader evaluation. Understand taxes, weigh them, but don't let the tax tail wag the investment dog. Ultimately, if your investments are successful, you'll make enough money to cover your taxes...and then some.

Question 1—

From a tax standpoint, the best investment option is:

a) Individual Retirement Accounts.

b) 401(k) plans.

c) Stocks.

d) Any of the above, depending on your tax situation and needs.

As with most aspects of investing, taxes usually involve trade-offs. You may, for example, enjoy the benefits of tax-free investments, but typically you must purchase these with after-tax dollars, meaning you've already paid taxes on the money invested. Tax-deferred assets allow you to delay taxes, but these come due when you begin taking distributions.

Thus, as you design your portfolio, it's essential to understand the tax consequences of each potential investment. The U.S. Tax Code establishes several categories of income, along with corresponding tax rates. These are:

Ordinary income

Most income falls into this category. It's taxed at the applicable rate in the IRS tables.

Interest and dividend income

No matter its source, interest and dividend income is considered ordinary income and taxed at the applicable rate.

Capital gains

Capital gains are those derived from the sale of certain assets, such as stocks, and may be treated at a more favorable tax rate than ordinary income. Just how favorably depends on how long you've held the asset. If you've owned it for less than one year, the capital gain is considered "short-term" and taxed as ordinary income—no break there. If you've owned it for more than one year, the appreciation is considered a "long-term" capital gain and taxed at a lower rate. If you own an investment for more than five years, an even lower capital gains tax is applied, provided the investment was acquired after the year 2000.

It's also important to note that capital gains can be offset by capital losses. For example, if sale of a stock brings you a capital gain of $1,000, sale of another stock at a loss of $1,000 will offset the capital gain and wipe out your tax obligation. All capital gains and losses are based on calendar-year transactions.

With this broad understanding of tax categories at your base, you can move on to consider the tax implications of each asset class and subclass. Here are a few examples that most investors must ponder from time to time:

Stocks

Because capital losses can be used to offset capital gains, many investors engage in year-end tax-planning, selling off certain stocks to realize the losses before the January 1 deadline. Sometimes, this is savvy planning. Yet be mindful of our dictum about taxes and investments—again, don't let the tax tail wag the investment dog. If you sell a security for tax-planning purposes, you may miss out when that stock experiences a growth spurt in the next year. Fundamental values and goal achievement should guide your buy/sell decisions, with tax considerations playing a supporting role.

Another reason to carefully pick your spots for year-end divestment: *wash sale rules.* Under the rules for wash sales, if you sell a security and want to declare a loss associated with that holding, you must wait 31 days before buying back that particular security. If you don't mind being out of that investment for at least 31 days, wash rules are no big deal. Still, they do represent a reason for year-round consideration of potential capital losses, rather than a rushed December sale that could keep you out of a stock for 31 days.

Taxable and tax-free municipal bonds

You can invest in bonds that require you to pay taxes on interest earned, or you can select bonds that provide interest tax-free. Sounds like a no-brainer, right? It isn't because tax-free bonds usually offer lower interest rates than do taxable bonds. Thus, to determine which of these assets is better for you, you must calculate what you would earn from each and what your tax obligation would be for each. It isn't complicated, but it's far from a no-brainer. It's yet another example of trade-offs in the world of investing.

Annuities

Annuities provide tax-deferred growth with a compounding effect over the years, so that's a plus. On the other hand, you buy annuities with after-tax dollars, so there's no immediate tax benefit. Also on the down side: earnings ultimately are taxed as ordinary income when withdrawn, and the IRS imposes a 10 percent penalty for withdrawals prior to age 59 1/2. Further, annuities don't receive a step-up in cost basis upon the owner's death, so your heirs are responsible for taxes on all the gains, which are considered ordinary income.

A general rule of thumb: The higher your tax bracket, the more likely you are to benefit from annuities because of the tax-deferred status of your gains.

Individual retirement accounts

We examined the most popular types of IRAs in some detail in Chapter 3, so here we'll focus on their tax characteristics.

- ▣ **Traditional IRAs.** With traditional IRAs, your contributions provide you with a tax deduction equal to the amount of your contribution; in effect, your contribution gains pre-tax status. The money in your account grows tax-deferred, making this IRA quite a useful tool. Withdrawals prior to age 59 1/2 are taxed and assessed a 10 percent penalty, although there are certain exceptions. Mandatory distributions begin at age 70 1/2, with taxes assessed according to your tax bracket.

- ▣ **Non-deductible IRAs.** The tax situation here is the same in most regards as with a traditional IRA, except you don't get a deduction for your current taxes. You're making contributions with after-tax dollars, but your earnings are tax-deferred. Mandatory distributions and early-withdrawal features are the same.

- ▣ **Roth IRAs.** Your contributions are made with after-tax dollars, so there's no immediate tax benefit, but your account grows tax-free. Roth IRAs have no mandatory distribution requirements; when you do decide to begin taking distributions, you do so without worrying about taxes.

401(k) Plans

Contributions here are with pre-tax dollars, so there are no taxes now on the money you contribute. Your contributions, some of which would otherwise go to the government as taxes, enjoy a compounding effect over time, a tremendous benefit to you. Throw in the employer "match"—if that's a feature of your plan—and you have a gift that keeps on giving.

Withdrawals prior to age 59 1/2 are taxed; in most cases, the IRS imposes a penalty of 10 percent as well. Mandatory distributions kick in at age 70 1/2, with taxes according to your tax bracket.

We made our case for the value of 401(k) plans in Chapter 3, so we won't belabor that case here. It's worth repeating, though, that active management of your 401(k) plan will maximize its benefit for you and help you avoid reliance on a single investment sector—that's what did in the Enron victims.

It's easy to be lulled into a false sense of security regarding 401(k) accounts because they're seemingly managed by our employers, which we generally regard as benevolent forces in our lives. Your employer may indeed be managing the overall plan, but it doesn't follow that your company is tending your particular account. The responsibility for active management is yours.

Once you understand the tax features of each asset, you'll be well-positioned to select those that are best suited for your situation. For example, investing all your money in a traditional IRA or a 401(k) plan will give you taxable proceeds at some point in your retirement and—if you anticipate having substantial additional income—perhaps propel you into a higher tax bracket. If that's the case with you, balancing your investments between a 401(k) account and a Roth IRA (provided you qualify), where distributions never are taxable, might be a useful approach. Whatever the specific mix works for you, you'll be able to pursue a tax-efficient investment program.

Scoring:

As we've seen, the tax properties of asset classes and subclasses vary—as does their impact on investors. Therefore, the best answer, worth 4 points, is d). Because certain asset classes may be particularly useful in your situation, score 3 points for b), 2 for a), 1 for c).

Question 2—

The best approach to payroll deductions is:

a) Minimize them wherever you can so you increase your take-home pay.

b) Maximize them wherever you can so you owe less in taxes come April 15.

c) Choose and monitor them carefully, selecting the best option for you in each case.

d) Don't sweat payroll deductions— what can you do about them anyway?

You can do a lot about payroll deductions—that's why we've included this question. Many people focus exclusively on the cash portion of their pay packages. But if you ignore your deductions, that may have an adverse impact on your financial situation over the long term.

Begin your considerations with the amount you designate for withholding—the amount withheld from your paycheck by your employer and sent directly to the Internal Revenue Service. (If you're self-employed, you handle your own withholding via quarterly estimated tax payments.) In effect, the federal government gathers taxes from you every pay period, rather than having to collect the entire amount from you annually. It works for the government, and it can work well for you as well. Many people find it easier to live without the small amount withheld from each paycheck than to produce an onerous tax payment each April 15.

The amount withheld is based, in part, upon the allowances you claimed on the W-4 form you completed when you were hired. You probably arrived at your initial designation in haste, when the HR director threw that intimidating new-hire packet at you. If you're like most of us, you indicated a withholding amount without much thought. It may seem like a small point to you even now—what difference does it make to your financial situation if you pay your taxes in one lump sump or through 26 or 52 small pieces of your salary? But there are some fairly important reasons to assure that your withholding is aligned with your income tax liability.

First, if you overestimate your tax obligation and have too much salary withheld, you're not utilizing your money wisely. Some folks prefer to maximize their withholding because it denies them access to money they would otherwise spend, and it helps provide a tax refund every year. But consider the downside. The IRS doesn't pay interest on overpayments. You could be investing the money you're overpaying in taxes. If you're maximizing withholding as a way of imposing discipline on yourself, try this approach instead: Reduce your withholding and earmark the difference for automatic contributions to your 401(k) account or other pension plan.

On the other hand, if you're not withholding enough, it could leave you with a substantial federal tax obligation, a financial penalty from the IRS for insufficient payments, or both. Penalties always are a useless expense. Thus, it makes a lot of sense to get your withholding right.

Next, consider deductions for such benefits as health, life, and disability insurance. We're always trying to escape as cheaply as possible with these to enhance our take-home pay, but is that really the way to go? If your company offers health insurance options, the temptation may be strong to select the cheapest option—especially if enrollment of dependents makes it a terribly expensive proposition for you. But the least expensive plan also may be the least flexible and the least comprehensive, failing to cover the specific medical needs of you and your family. Study all options carefully. You may find investing in a more expensive plan is a better approach to your long-term health. That's a worthy trade-off.

Make the same informed decisions on life and disability insurance. Because employers typically enjoy discounted rates from insurers, they're able to offer you participation rather cheaply. But the coverage may be seriously limited and far less than you actually need.

What happens if you lose your job? This is hardly a rare phenomenon in today's economy. We've seen it befall a client, and it isn't pretty. He had never supplemented his company-provided insurance with a private plan. Then, after suffering the blow of downsizing, he found that no life insurer would offer him coverage because he was experiencing health problems. The double-barreled attack left him without any life insurance to protect his family, and no real recourse for getting any.

The lesson to be learned here is that it's fine to load up on company-provided insurance, but only if you use it to supplement coverage that you purchase on the open market. Sure, this will adversely affect your finances now, but you and your family never will lose protection through career dislocation.

Finally, think about your 401(k) plan contributions, if you are offered such a program at work. After the Enron debacle, many concerned workers dropped their 401(k) participation in favor of investing outside the plan. Remember that your

401(k) contributions are with *before-tax dollars*. If you take money from your paycheck and invest it, you're buying less than you could have with pre-tax 401(k) contributions.

Here's a concrete example of what we mean. Let's suppose your federal income tax rate is 25 percent. If you invest $100 in a 401(k) plan, you're investing the full $100 because you pay no taxes on that $100. But if you choose to invest $100 after you receive your paycheck, you'll really have only $75 to invest because you must pay $25 in taxes. You could opt to keep your investment level at $100, but that would mean an outlay of $133—$100 invested, about $33 for taxes. There's no doubt that 401(k) plans continue to make sense, provided you manage them actively and effectively.

We've all experienced the disappointment that comes when deductions create the Amazing Disappearing Paycheck. Yet an ill-conceived determination to limit those deductions could have disastrous effects over the long term. Let your long-term well-being, not the size of your take-home pay, drive your deduction decisions.

Scoring:

Choosing the right tax and benefits options at work can be a vital part of your investment plan, so score 4 points for c), 0 for any other answer.

Question 3—

Which of the following is the formula used to calculate the cost basis for mutual funds?

a) Original purchase + additional contributions + reinvested dividends + reinvested capital gains.

b) Original purchase + additional contributions + distributed dividends + reinvested capital gains.

c) Original purchase + additional contributions + reinvested dividends + distributed capital gains.

d) Original purchase + additional contributions + distributed dividends + distributed capital gains.

When we discussed the tax features of certain asset classes and subclasses in Question 1, we deliberately omitted mutual funds for the time being, because the tax situation for such funds is more complex.

To calculate the cost basis of a mutual fund—the starting point for tax calculations—begin with the original investment, then add the value of all additional purchases and all dividends and capital gains that have been reinvested. Dividends and capital gains are treated the same as additional purchases. Whether you take your dividends and capital gains in cash or reinvest them in the fund, it's a taxable event.

Also, if the share price of a mutual fund declines through the course of a year but the fund pays dividends and capital gains, you're still responsible for taxes on the dividends and capital gains. This happened to many investors in the first few years of this century. They reinvested rather than pocketed their distributions, saw their investments lose ground overall, and still ended up with a tax obligation. This may seem like insult heaped upon injury, but there is a benefit down the road when you sell the fund and finally get to restore to your cost basis the value of all the dividends and capital gains you reinvested, because you've already paid taxes on that money. Here is an example:

Original investment	$10,000	
Reinvested dividends	$ 500	
Reinvested capital gains	$ 1,000	
Sale proceeds		$11,000
Cost basis	$11,500	
Net gain (loss)		($500)

In this scenario, you invest $10,000 in a mutual fund and reinvest $500 in dividends and $1,000 in capital gains—paying taxes on the dividends and capital gains. When you sell the fund for $11,000, you get to add the reinvested dividends and capital gains to the cost basis, providing you a net loss for tax purposes of $500. In reality, you enjoy a profit of $1,000—$11,000 in sale proceeds less the $10,000 out-of-pocket investment—minus the taxes you paid. But because your reinvested dividends and capital gains become part of the cost basis, you're able to produce a capital loss that can help offset capital gains. It should be noted that keeping good records is essential in understanding the tax consequences of your mutual fund investments.

Even beyond this, unrealized capital gains can be the hidden joker in the mutual funds deck. Consider this scenario. You invest in the Get Rich Quick Fund (GRQF), which has been holding Microsoft since its initial public offering. Just after you make your purchase, GRQF decides to sell its entire Microsoft holdings, creating a sizable capital gain—a portion of which is allocated to you. You weren't in the fund during Microsoft's huge run-up, you received no benefits from its spectacular rise, but as a new GRQF shareholder, you'll likely receive a taxable capital gains distribution.

There are some measures you can take to better understand this potential tax exposure with mutual funds. First, a number of research services—Morningstar is among the most popular—prepare and offer reports on mutual funds that include the value of unrealized or undistributed capital gains as well as the turnover rate. The higher the turnover rate, the higher the potential tax bill for shareholders.

And as you research, make sure you note when funds are due to make their dividend and capital gains distributions. That will help you avoid investing right before the distribution, which would create a taxable event for you without adding any value. Some investors make the mistake of jumping in right before the distribution, thinking that will provide them with an instant benefit. They receive the distribution (and corresponding tax obligation), but the share price is readjusted to reflect the distribution. In effect, they gain nothing but a tax bill.

While some of the tax features of mutual funds may seem unfair, there is an upside. With stocks, you may be tempted to hang on to a security for too long because you don't want to trigger the tax obligation that comes with a sale. Mutual funds and their periodic distributions are more of a pay-as-you-go system. Because you're paying some taxes along the way, the ultimate bite may not be as deep.

Scoring:

Score 4 points for a), 0 for any other answer.

Question 4—

Owning a home can be good for your long-term financial health because:

a) You acquire an asset that may appreciate in value.

b) Mortgage interest and certain home-related expenses might be tax-deductible.

c) Your home can be the foundation of successful retirement.

d) All of the above.

You may wonder why we're addressing your living arrangements in a book about investing. For many people, purchasing a home will be the most important investment they ever make. If you plan and execute your purchase well, it could leave you in a solid and secure financial position, providing the wherewithal for investments in other assets. Done ineffectively, home-buying can be a tremendous drain on assets and leave little additional money for investing. That's why it's important to spend some time considering your living arrangements.

Most of us have grown up with the old bromide that owning is better than renting. For many, this will be true, for a number of reasons. Typically, mortgage interest and home-improvement expenses qualify as deductions if they're itemized on your federal income tax return. Without them, many taxpayers don't bother itemizing their deductions and end up paying more taxes than they might need to. So home-related deductions are valuable of themselves while serving as a gateway to the full range of itemized deductions.

With ownership, you also build equity that you can use for a variety of purposes. Your home may be growing in value, enabling you to sell it someday at a handsome profit. On the other hand, if you have no desire to sell, you can live in your dwelling long after you've paid off the mortgage—saving considerably on living expenses. These savings may be your admission to early retirement.

Many potential homebuyers believe, incorrectly, that they can't afford mortgage payments and so elect to rent instead. Before you make that choice, consider this example. You have the option to rent for $700 per month or to purchase a home that would produce $10,000 in tax deductions. If you're in the

28 percent tax bracket, those deductions will save you $2,800—$233 per month over a year's time—in federal income taxes. Thus, a monthly mortgage payment of $933 actually is the equivalent of $700 in monthly rent when tax deductions are factored in. In this case, you can go house hunting secure in the knowledge that any monthly mortgage payment less than $933 will be cheaper than renting for $700 per month—plus you get all the other benefits of home ownership.

With so many financial institutions offering mortgages, it's a great time to shop for the best value. That means the interest rate, of course, but it also means the term of the loan, the down payment requirement and all the subtle expenses, such as origination points and closing costs. We call these subtle because few lenders like to discuss them. Compare all aspects of the proposed mortgage package to get the best deal.

Today's attractive mortgage interest rates also raise the possibility of refinancing an existing loan. If you're thinking about refinancing your mortgage, our advice is to do so when your new loan package brings you lower monthly rates without adding to your term. Lower rates may not help much if to get them, you must add 10 or 20 years to your repayment schedule. Even with the lower payments, you may be starting from scratch in writing down your debt, and you may be pushing retirement further into the future. If you're able to achieve lower payments *and* an accelerated repayment schedule through refinancing, that's the deal you want. You pay less per month, and for a shorter period. Jump on that one!

It remains true that some people will opt for renting because they fear the expense—and unpredictable expense at that—of home ownership. If you understand the financial trade-offs and still determine that renting works best for you, do so without guilt or shame. There's no need to join a support group. *(Hi. My name is Bob, and I'm a renter.)* You've made the best financial decision for your situation, and that's what successful investing is about.

Scoring:

Score 4 points for d), but give yourself 2 points for any other answer. All are benefits of home ownership.

Question 5—

To preserve as much of your estate as possible, you should:

a) Take it with you.

b) Begin a gifting program now.

c) Explore trusts to help shelter assets from estate taxes.

d) All of the above.

When you invest, your immediate goal is to build wealth for use in your lifetime. But many investors have a second important objective—to create an estate to bequeath to beneficiaries, whether they are immediate family, friends, or favorite causes. Indeed, ensuring that the needs of our loved ones are met after our passing may become a primary goal of investing, rather than a subordinate goal. That's why understanding and dealing with estate taxes is an important element of your investing program. If you're effective in this area, you'll preserve as much of your estate as possible while meeting all your tax obligations.

The area of estate taxes is, in a word, fluid. Until rather recently, the federal tax bite on inherited property was crushing; assets greater than $675,000 were taxed at rates ranging from 37 percent to 55 percent. The burden was so severe that many heirs were forced to sell the family businesses they inherited just to meet their tax bills.

Congress addressed the matter with the Economic Growth and Tax Relief Reconciliation Act of 2001, which phases out the federal estate tax. In 2010, the tax is scheduled to disappear completely. The problem is that the Tax Relief Act "sunsets" in 2011; in that year, its provisions become null and avoid. Absent further congressional action, the estate tax reappears, in all its crushing glory, after the sunset.

This uncertain situation is complicated by other factors, including the pending elimination of the "stepped up" cost basis for inheritances. Prior to the Tax Relief Act, when heirs received property, the corresponding cost basis was equal to the market value of the asset on the decedent's date of death. Therefore, when the inherited assets were sold by the heir, capital gains taxes were minimized. This was a tremendous benefit—especially if the asset had appreciated significantly. Alas, this benefit is going away in 2010 on assets over $1.3 million for nonspousal transfers, over $4.3 million for spousal transfers. Assets over these limits will retain their original cost basis and generate potentially significant capital gains taxes.

Taxes also loom large in any individual retirement accounts or 401(k) plans that you've been funding on a tax-deferred basis. If you die before taking distributions and paying taxes on your gains, that tax burden will fall on your heirs. Think of the potential growth in these plans over 20 or 30 years and you begin to see the scope of the problem.

You can add to all this the near inevitability of state inheritance taxes. The phase-out of federal estate taxes does nothing to cushion the blow of state levies, which vary across a wide range. Some states impose stiff taxes while others have milder taxes with generous exemptions. If you're familiar with the inheritance taxes in your state, you'll be better able to plan for them.

In this unsettled situation, your estate continues to be at risk, so it makes sense to engage in estate planning now. Here are several key steps to consider:

Begin a gifting program.

This is as simple as it sounds—you give part of your estate to your beneficiaries now, rather than post-mortem. Gifting programs remove assets from your name, thereby reducing the size of your taxable estate and decelerating the estate's growth. You don't trigger gift taxes as long as your gifts are no more than $11,000 per person, per year; the compounding effect of your gifts can be substantial.

If you do consider a gifting program, don't conceive it as a hurried, short-term ploy to diminish your estate and better qualify for Medicaid support that can make a nursing home more avoidable. Under Medicaid eligibility rules, any outright gifts you've made over the past three years, and gifts to trusts over the last five years, are considered part of your estate. Thanks to these look-back rules, "instant gifting" can serve to delay your receipt of Medicaid benefits. Instead, think of gifting as a long-term program that you begin now.

Explore the advantages of trusts.

Trusts can protect a significant portion of your estate from taxes. One of the most useful of these tools is the *bypass trust*, which enables couples to take full advantage of the *unified credit*—the amount that can be passed to your heirs without federal estate taxes. The 2002 exemption limit of $1 million increases to $3.5 million by the year 2009 before being fully repealed in 2010.

Only assets titled individually can be allocated to a bypass trust. To maximize the benefit, the value of assets in each spouse's name should be equal to the unified credit amount, assuming there are sufficient assets. It's in your interest to pay close attention to the annual increases in the exemption limit outlined in the Tax Relief Act of 2001. As with the federal estate tax, the exemption limit will revert to its 2001 level of $675,000 without further action by Congress.

As you explore this area, you'll discover other trusts that can help you in estate planning. Some trusts are designed to transfer your residence or other specific assets to your heirs. Others provide you with immediate income and tax advantages while establishing charitable organizations as the ultimate beneficiaries. *In trusts, we trust* might be a good motto for your estate planning.

Keep thorough records.

Knowing the cost basis for each asset—and keeping the documentation accessible—won't help your beneficiaries avoid applicable taxes, but it will help you and your heirs with estate planning. It will cut the time and costs in settling your estate, even as it minimizes potential problems with the IRS.

Scoring:

Score 4 points for b) or c). If you answered a), score 1 point for your inventiveness...and please contact us immediately to let us know how you intend to take it with you. We want in.

	Scoring for Chapter 11	
	Highest Possible Score	**Your Score**
Question 1	4	_____
Question 2	4	_____
Question 3	4	_____
Question 4	4	_____
Question 5	4	_____
CHAPTER TOTALS	20	_____

12 The Costs of Investing and Portfolio Management— You Thought It Was Free?

We've all grown up with the homily, "You get what you pay for." Most of us readily accept this as the wisdom of the ages...until it comes to financial planning and portfolio management. Then, we forget all about the old saw and try to tame the investment beast ourselves, or hire the cheapest advisor we can find. But in the investment area, friends, you get what you pay for.

Think of it another way. Surveys consistently show persuasively that our top three concerns are family, health, and money, although the order may vary from person to person. When your family needs it, you bring in all the professional help you can afford. When you're sick, you see a doctor rather than trying to heal yourself. So why is it that some people are confident they can handle the third key area, money, without expert advice?

The answer may have something to do with the availability of information. So much of it is out there—on broadcast and cable television, in subscription newsletters, on the Web—that the sheer volume of data convinces investors they know everything they need to know. But information is not the same as knowledge. Information is not the same as experience. You need both knowledge and experience to succeed at investing.

As we've stressed throughout this book, successful portfolio management requires broad understanding of economics, investments, tax and estate laws, finance, accounting—and a little math aptitude doesn't hurt. Yes, managing your own portfolio is possible, if you're able to commit sufficient time to the task. It will become something like a full-time hobby. Take it from folks in the business. There's always one more article that you must read, one more new investment option that you must understand, one more financial statement or prospectus that you must analyze.

Unless you're prepared for this hostile takeover of your life, you're better off allocating your extra time to the pursuit of your career and maximizing your income rather than trying to manage a field as complex as investing. If you engage a professional manager to help you invest wisely, you'll likely be more successful than if you do it yourself—even when you factor in the management fees you're paying.

If you decide to engage a professional manager, you'll want to understand how people get paid in this industry. Costs here are tricky. They take such forms as fees, commissions, 12(b)-1 fees, expense ratios, administrative costs, and loads. Our next series of questions will help you gauge your understanding of these fees and other aspects of outside portfolio management.

One final point: While we usually recommend professional portfolio management, we're not suggesting that you abandon your active role in your own financial planning. It remains your job to learn as much as you can, so that when your portfolio manager presents you with recommendations and options, you'll be prepared to make the decisions that best advance your goals.

Question 1—

In the investing world, "load" is best defined as:

a) Your asset allocation formula.

b) The commission you pay when buying shares in a mutual fund.

c) Your brother-in-law, with his pesky financial advice.

d) All of the above.

As noted, mutual funds offer many advantages, but they also bring costs that typically aren't well understood by investors. The most basic of these costs is the *load*, a synonym for *commission*. All funds are described as either load, because they charge a commission, or no-load, because there is no commission.

With a load fund, most of the commission is used to compensate your brokerage firm and the advisor providing you with counsel and servicing your account. The balance of the load is retained by the mutual fund to help cover expenses. No-load funds are available for investors making their own fund purchases; do-it-yourselfers aren't receiving professional advice, so these funds don't tack on the load.

Some investors who manage their own portfolios make the classic mistake of buying load funds, in effect paying for advice they're not getting. This is akin to selling your home yourself, then walking into your neighborhood real-estate office and voluntarily paying the agent a commission. There's no point to this. You may find a load fund so attractive that it seems worth an unearned commission, but there are plenty of no-load funds that may work just as well.

In a given load fund, loads are not uniformly assessed. Rather, they're often assigned differently to different classes of shares. If a fund has three classes of shares, these typically are designated Class A, Class B, and Class C. While that's the standard typology, you'll also find share classes with more exotic lettering. Should you encounter Class M or Class Z shares, it's best to check the prospectus for the details. Here's a look at the common share classes:

Class A shares

These usually carry up-front loads ranging from 4 percent to 5 percent. However, you won't see the load itemized on your transaction confirmation. An itemized confirmation would specify all the categories, such as: Investment, $100,000; Commission, $4,750; Value, $95,250. At a glance, you would know the commission paid and the beginning value of your investment. Would that it were so simple.

Instead, you purchase the fund at the "offering price" and sell it at the "net asset value," or NAV, as it's known. Unless you review the prospectus and understand the load involved, you may not even realize you were hit with a commission.

It's crucial to understand loads. Consider the example of a fund with a 4 percent load, relatively modest as they go. The first 4 percent growth in your fund will do nothing more for you than make up for the commission you paid. This is quite achievable in a growth fund that might take off quickly. But in a bond fund with a 4 percent load, recouping your commission may be a more laborious process. If the bond fund is generating 4 percent annual growth, it will take you more than a year just to recapture your commission.

With Class A shares, most mutual funds offer *breakpoints*—discounts on the load to reward certain levels of investment. For example, if you invest $100,000 or less, your load may be 5 percent. Invest from $100,000 to $200,000 and your load may drop to 4.5 percent. The discounts can get deeper as the investment increases. In fact, many funds waive the load outright for investments of $1 million or more. Moreover, you typically can reach a breakpoint by combining all your investments within the same mutual fund family—still another benefit of portfolio diversification.

If you plan on investing enough over 13 months to reach a breakpoint, many mutual funds will require you to sign a letter of intent to qualify for the load discount. Should you fail to reach your stated goal, they'll assess the appropriate load after 13 months.

Class B shares

With this class of shares, the commission typically is charged at the back end. You purchase shares at NAV; your load depends on when you sell. For example, if a fund has a five-year back-end load, it may charge 5 percent if you liquidate in the first year, 4 percent in the second year, 3 percent in the third year, 2 percent in the fourth year, 1 percent in the fifth year, and nothing thereafter.

Many funds permit limited withdrawals—typically between 8 percent and 12 percent of your holdings—without assessing the back-end load. In addition, some funds don't charge the load on earnings.

Class C shares

In Class C, the load is assessed annually, rather than at the time of purchase or sale. A common Class C annual load is 1 percent.

Which class of shares you choose can depend on your goals and time frame. If you intend to hold your investment for, say, 15 years, you probably wouldn't opt for Class C; over that long a period, your 1 percent annual load could far exceed the up-front or back-end commission you would pay with the other classes. In this situation, Class B shares would appear to make more sense, since you could end up with no load at all.

Yet there are other factors at play here—chiefly the expense ratios of the funds you're targeting. It's vital to understand and compare expense ratios since fund expenses affect fund performance. The higher the costs, the better the fund must perform to overcome its outsized expenses.

All mutual funds have expense ratios, which include all costs for running the fund. Administrative and management expenses as well as trading costs are captured in the expense ratio. So are marketing expenses, including a category known as 12(b)-1 fees. These may be the most controversial of the costs because they include fees paid to your investment advisor—and all other portfolio managers who keep their clients in the fund.

Some observers believe that 12(b)-1 fees raise the specter of conflicts of interest, since your portfolio manager receives the fee only as long as you stay in the fund. If your manager recommends that you stay in, how can you tell if that advice is inspired primarily by the desire to keep the 12(b)-1 fees flowing?

This is a legitimate concern of which all mutual fund investors must be mindful. On the plus side, 12(b)-1 fees don't come directly out of your pocket, and they do give your portfolio manager a stake in your investment success, a feature that shouldn't be diminished. (We'll discuss remuneration approaches for professional advisors below.) The most important point about 12(b)-1 fees is that they're included in expense ratios—not a separate cost in addition to expense ratios—so you always have the opportunity to study and evaluate them. Don't get hung up on 12(b)-1 fees. For our money, we'd much rather pay for professional portfolio monitoring than underwrite national TV spots that can cost millions. Advertising may help the fund, but it does zip for our account.

Expense ratios vary with the type of fund. Growth funds, with their high turnover rates, weigh in with an average expense ratio of 1.55 percent. For bond funds, the average expense ratio is appreciably lower at 0.95 percent. When you explore expense ratios, don't look at them in a vacuum. Instead, evaluate them relative to performance. If a fund boasts a superior track record but carries a slightly higher-than-average expense ratio, the additional costs may be worth it. But if a higher expense ratio can't be justified by performance, you may want to look elsewhere.

A final point to remember about expense ratios is that your share class also can be a factor in the percentage of fund expenses you pay. The expense ratio for Class B shares always is higher than it is for Class A shares. Remember that with Class B shares, the fund doesn't collect a commission from you until you sell, yet it continues to incur expenses. So it bumps up the expense ratio for Class B shares to help make up the difference.

After a number of years—usually at the close of the period when you're subject to a deferred load—the fund may convert your B shares to A shares to allow you to enjoy the lower expense ratio. They're reasoning is: *Okay, we've collected enough extra money from you to compensate for the absence of an up-front commission, so now we'll let you move to the lower-expense class of shares.*

The performance of Class A shares always will be marginally better than that of Class B shares of the same fund—the typical difference is about 0.5 percent. Yet studies have shown that there isn't much long-term difference between these two share classes. With Class A shares, less money goes to work for you at a slightly higher return. With Class B shares, 100 percent of your money goes to work for you at a slightly lower return. Your objectives and cash flow needs will determine which share class works best for you.

Scoring:

Score 4 points for b), 0 for any other answer.
By the way, you're not taking your brother-in-law's advice, are you?

Question 2—

When you purchase bonds through a broker, the broker's commission is called:

a) Juice.

b) Nick.

c) Mark-up.

d) Vigorish.

When you buy individual stocks or bonds (as opposed to those in a mutual fund) through a broker, the broker or other professional usually charges a *commission*. For individual stock trades, the commission is added on to the price of the stock. It's a straightforward add-on; when you review the transaction confirmation, you can easily differentiate the stock price from the commission.

The same isn't true with the purchase of individual bonds. Here, the broker typically charges a commission called a *mark-up*, meaning that the commission is built into the price of the bond. You don't see any additional charge, which leads some investors to believe they don't pay commissions on bond transactions. But you do, and you're best advised to determine the broker's commission before authorizing the purchase. Ask your broker about the mark-up—and don't hesitate to comparison shop. If your broker isn't providing you with advice as well as transaction services, there may be little reason to use that broker's service and incur full commissions as a result. In that case, you can buy and sell on your own, employing a discount broker to save on commissions.

While you're considering commissions and mark-up rates of the brokers you survey, consider several other aspects of their services as well. If you've been using a broker for awhile, check out the *execution prices*—the actual prices of the transactions they've been getting for you. Some brokers have a better capability for quick execution on the floor of the exchange.

Perhaps you want to buy a stock when it reaches $16, but your broker dallies and doesn't complete the deal until the share price reaches $16.50. That costs you money that can add up with a large volume of transactions. Make sure your broker jumps on your orders when you place them—that's the service for which you're paying.

If you're looking to your broker for services beyond buying and selling, make sure you inquire about those. Will your broker provide you with financial planning guidance? Portfolio monitoring and management? If so, how will the broker be remunerated beyond commissions?

Also, remember that, as 12(b)-1 fees, broker commissions introduce the possibility of conflicts of interest. Is your broker recommending a trade simply to pocket the commission or because it's in your best interest? If you can't trust your broker's objectivity, you can't trust your broker.

Scoring:

Score 4 points for c), 0 for any other answer. If you answered a), b), or d), 'fess up. You've been gambling in some venue other than the stock market.

Question 3—

Asset managers and financial planners typically employ which of these compensation structures?

a) Fee only.

b) Commission-based.

c) Fee and commissions.

d) Any or all of the above.

As we've seen, fees and costs in the investment arena are varied and not always easy to discern. Yet another cost is the price of financial planning or asset management. While the range of fees can be broad, how compensation is structured may be a more important distinction.

One factor involved is the type of services that you purchase. If your consultant is providing financial planning only—that is, you're making the transactions yourself based on your consultant's recommendations—that may lead to one type of compensation structure. If you're purchasing both financial planning and brokering services, compensation may be addressed differently.

Here's a look at some of the most common fee structures:

Asset management fees (Wrap accounts)

In this scenario, brokers or financial planners charge a percentage of your assets to manage your portfolio. Some will include other financial planning services in their management fees—as close as this industry gets to a comprehensive fee. Others may charge an additional fee for financial planning.

A typical fee for portfolio management is 1 percent, but your asset mix can affect the charge. For example, if your account consists primarily of fixed-income assets, the fee may be lower—0.6 percent or less. If your account is heavy on individual stocks, the fee may range to 1.5 percent to compensate your advisor for the additional research involved.

Once the fee is established, you shouldn't be paying any commissions or loads. You may have administrative expenses such as ticket charges, which commonly run about $20 per trade. And your broker or advisor may be garnering 12(b)-1 fees from the mutual funds in your portfolio. Typically, advisors who earn such commissions charge a lower asset management fee.

But all your purchases should be at NAV. Most mutual funds allow investment advisors to waive the load within a wrap account. Thus, your advisor should do just that—waive the load—and purchase the class of shares with the lowest expense ratio. If you're paying an asset management fee *and* loads, your advisor is double dipping, an intolerable and inexcusable situation.

Wrap accounts bring a number of advantages. First, it's a pay as-you-go system—you typically pay your fee on a quarterly basis. You're not forking over huge up-front commissions only to discover after spending all that money that your advisor isn't providing the service you want. To keep you as a satisfied client, your advisor must actively service the account. And because your advisor doesn't earn a commission on each sale, you'll know that any changes recommended should be in your best interest. No conflict of interest concerns here.

Wrap accounts also provide you and your advisor with the flexibility to make changes as necessary without being restricted by commission costs. A true asset allocation approach—something recommended throughout this book—requires regular portfolio balancing, which in turn means regular asset sales and purchases. If you aren't in an asset management account, the commissions associated with asset allocation can erode your returns.

This also brings a downside in the form of greater taxes. Frequent buying and selling in a taxable account, as opposed to a tax-free or tax-deferred retirement account, will generate frequent tax bills. This, too, is a common feature of wrap accounts but not a cause for alarm. As previously noted, you should be aware of the tax consequences of your investments without letting them drive your decisions.

Commission-based

With this structure, advisors earn the bulk of their compensation via commission. They may charge an additional nominal fee for financial planning or analysis.

Fee-only

Fee-only advisors don't earn commissions but charge either a flat fee or an hourly fee. Many fee-only planners don't implement transactions for you; they'll do so if you ask, but they may charge an additional fee for implementing and monitoring.

A word of caution about hourly fees: these are quite legitimate, but some investors find it irritating to know that each conversation with their advisors will generate billable time. The danger is that you won't seek that advice because it will result in additional expense. If hourly fees would inhibit the free flow of ideas between you and your advisor, this billing approach might not be for you.

Fee-based

In this category are advisors who charge a fee but have the ability to earn commissions. Many financial professionals who charge an asset management fee but also pick up trailing commissions are considered to be fee-based.

Fee and commission

Advisors in this category charge a fee to prepare a financial plan but may pick up additional compensation from transactions.

While we're partial to the asset management approach for the reasons noted above, any compensation structure can work provided you and your advisor are mutually comfortable with it and it helps you achieve your goals.

Scoring:

Score 4 points for d), 2 points for any other answer, since a), b), and c) all are commonly used compensation structures.

Question 4—

The best way to find a financial advisor or asset manager is:

a) Word of mouth followed by research.

b) Responding to cold calls.

c) The Yellow Pages and other forms of advertising.

d) Recommendations from financial trade organizations.

As seen in Question 3, compensation structure is one way to differentiate financial advisors, yet fee is far from your only consideration in selecting a professional to help you. It's easy to imagine a situation where you're paying less but not getting the service you want—not ideal circumstances when growing wealth is your objective. So it's critical to identify the right financial professional for your needs.

That sometimes is easier said than done. In a given day, you may encounter four or five advertisements for money management firms. In their hype, these souls all sound like the Mother Teresa of money management: outstanding track records, compassion, they satisfy us one client at a time and blah blah blah. How they survive serving one client at a time is beyond us. I guess we're not cut out for the ad biz.

Much of this is eyewash, yet the firms doing the advertising may well be strong, legitimate, and worthy of your consideration. If you hear something interesting in an ad, check it out. Let it inspire you to research the companies involved and their claims. But never accept it at face value.

Give the cold shoulder to cold calls as well. This is one of the most mystifying of phenomena in the financial landscape. Here's someone you've never met, never heard of, asking you to entrust your entire personal fortune based on a single cold call. It's hard to imagine anyone's agreeing to do that, and yet the cold callers keep calling; they wouldn't do that if the technique weren't successful. It never should snare you. Feel no compunction about hanging up on these hustlers. You don't owe them a second of your time—or a penny of your fortune.

Word of mouth, on the other hand, is a reasonable way to identify candidates for your business. It's an instant and often unsolicited referral from a friend or relative who has nothing to gain by offering the recommendation. If you can identify several candidates through word of mouth, you'll be well-positioned to follow up with the research that's essential in selecting your professional.

After you compile a list of candidates, call them to schedule appointments; they'll be only too happy to see you. Schedule your visits for their offices rather than a neutral site, such as lunch at a local restaurant. That will give you an opportunity to inspect their facilities and get a handle on staff size, equipment used, and other factors that you can't gauge on neutral turf. Once you're there, include these areas in your discussion:

Fees and scope of services

You have some ideas now of how compensation can be shaped. Explore fee options, and make sure you understand what services your money will be buying. Will your professional be a planner? A broker? Both? Is there additional compensation for transactions? Now is the time to ask.

If a candidate offers you a wrap account, make sure you understand the length of the commitment you're being asked to make. A one-year engagement makes sense; it would be hard to evaluate your advisor's performance in any period shorter than that. A three-year commitment may be too long, as it would tend to limit your ability to modify or end the relationship.

Credentials

Is your potential advisor a Certified Financial Planner? CFPs are educated in all areas of financial planning and typically provide well-rounded advice. If your candidate is a CFP, that's a strong plus.

You may encounter such other credentials as Chartered Financial Consultant (ChFC), Chartered Life Underwriter (CLU), and Chartered Financial Analyst (CFA). Make sure you understand what each certificate means, and if that expertise will help you meet your goals.

Investment philosophy

You must be comfortable with the basic philosophy of your advisor. Does your candidate try to time the market or favor a long-term, asset-allocation approach? How will your candidate respond to market declines? What mistakes has your prospect made in the past? Probe all these areas.

Personnel

While your interview may be with the CEO, that top executive may personally manage only a handful of accounts— and yours may not be one of them. Find out if your business will be assigned to another professional on staff, and make sure you meet with that person as well. Even if you hit it off with the CEO, assuring the right chemistry between you and your account manager may be more important.

Communication

How—and how often—will you communicate with your advisor? Will it be primarily by phone? By e-mail? This is something you need to know sooner rather than later. There's nothing more frustrating than wanting to make a trade, only to have your phone call to your broker go unreturned for several days. Establish a communication protocol as soon as possible.

Also remember our caution about hourly fees, which may keep you from initiating conversations for fear of generating billable time.

Review procedures

How will your financial plan be reviewed? Your circumstances will change; your portfolio must change as well. Regular meetings with your financial advisor are essential to review performance and initiate changes. Determine up front if your candidate returns phone calls promptly, has the support staff to monitor your portfolio and initiate contacts with you, and is amenable to regular meetings with you.

Other clients

Most prospects will provide you with the names of current customers; inevitably, those customers will offer glowing reviews of the advisors. There is a self-serving aspect to customer referrals, but it still makes sense to use them. You can gain some understanding of the advisor's services and approach from an existing client.

Finally, even as you interview candidates, make sure that they're interviewing you as well. The best relationships in the financial arena are *partnerships*. Your partner isn't there only to pluck off commissions. Your partner knows and understands your goals, carefully monitors your portfolio, and advises you on the best ways to achieve your objectives.

Your prospective advisor should be trying to learn about who you are, your financial goals, and risk tolerance. After all, professional advisors need to establish a comfort level as well. If there aren't any questions coming your way, you may want to move along to the next candidate.

Scoring:

Score 4 points for a), 0 for b) or c). Some financial trade organizations offer recommendations, but they may charge a fee for placement on their referral list, and their screening processes can be unreliable. Nevertheless, this is an option, so give yourself 2 points for d).

	Scoring for Chapter 12	
	Highest Possible Score	**Your Score**
Question 1	4	_____
Question 2	4	_____
Question 3	4	_____
Question 4	4	_____
CHAPTER TOTALS	16	_____

13 Exotica—Don't Try These at Home, Kids

C ash, stocks, bonds—and real estate, if you like—are the basic asset classes, although as we've seen, there are many subclasses that we need to understand before launching our investment programs. Yet veteran investors sometimes stray far afield from the standard fare into territory that is far more exotic and, often, far more speculative.

These high fliers often land on "derivatives," securities whose prices and movements are based on some other investment. They derive their value—thus the term *derivative*—from that base security, but themselves have no intrinsic value and therefore can't be liquidated.

Imagine that you go to the racetrack and bet on a horse. You get a paper ticket that you can convert to cash if your horse wins. But whether the horse succeeds or fails, you own no piece of the animal. The value of your ticket derives solely from the performance of the horse. Betting on horses is risky. So is investing in derivatives because you're buying assets with no core value.

The next series of questions will introduce you to some of this investment exotica. Don't take inclusion of these possibilities as a recommendation to participate. You should review them because it's common for financial reporters and newsletters to discuss such matters as options and the commodities market. However superficial these reports may be, they may tempt you to wade in. Resist that temptation until you're thoroughly grounded in all the scenarios and risks.

Question 1—

Which of these are not terms associated with *options*?

a) Puts and calls.

b) Buttons and bows.

c) Strips and straps.

d) Straddles and spreads.

The most popular form of derivative, options are based on stocks and resemble stock transactions in some ways, because they feature buyers and sellers. From there, the departure is dramatic.

Options, which represent claims on the underlying stocks, come in the forms of *puts* and *calls*. With calls, the buyer has the right or option to buy a certain number of shares of the stock involved at a specific price, called the *strike price* or *exercise*, before a certain date, known as the *expiration date*. The person selling the option, called the *writer*, earns a premium (payment) for providing the option. Premiums are market-driven—they are different for each transaction—but they are typically in the neighborhood of several dollars per share.

That's a lot of new terminology, so let's consider a specific example: an Acme Inc. six-month call option at $80 per share.

This option gives the buyer of the call the right to purchase a specified number of Acme shares at the strike price of $80 per share at any time during the six months before the expiration date. To honor the contract, the writer of the option must sell Acme stock that the writer already owns (called a *covered option*) or purchase Acme shares to sell to the buyer (considered a *naked option*).

Puts work the other way. Here, the buyer has the option to sell a certain number of shares at the strike price at any time before the expiration date. Per the agreement, the seller must purchase those shares if the buyer chooses, but the seller earns a premium as in call transactions.

There are covered and naked versions of puts as well. If the put writer has a "short" position in the stock involved, and therefore will profit if the stock declines, it's a covered option. If the seller has no short position in the stock involved, it's a naked option.

If you're the writer of options, whether you're covered or naked can make a world of difference. Once you have stock— or a short position that enables you to purchase that stock— your potential loss is finite. Whether the value of the stock rises or falls, you're covered if the option is exercised. Naked options leave the seller exposed, if you will.

Go back to our example of an Acme Inc. six-month call option at $80 per share. Now imagine that the option is for 1,000 shares and that during those six months, Acme shares explode to a trading value of $160, double the strike price. If the buyer calls the option at $160 and you're naked, that is, you're not holding any Acme stock that appreciated in value to $160, you must buy 1,000 shares on the open market for a total of $160,000. Since you're getting only $80,000 from the buyer (1,000 shares times the $80 strike price), you're out a quick $80,000 minus the premium, which won't be much against your huge loss. And of course, there's no reason why Acme shares would peak at $160; they might soar higher still. With naked options, your potential loss is inestimable.

A dangerous game, indeed, yet some investors feel they understand options well enough to take or minimize the risks. Here are some common options strategies:

Buying calls

Investors purchase calls when they think the price of a stock will increase. If it does, the buyer calls the stock from the writer at the strike price and sells it at the higher price, the current value of the stock. If the value of the stock declines over the option period, the buyer lets the option expire; the loss is limited to the premium paid to the writer.

If you anticipate growth in a stock, why would you buy a call rather than the stock itself? The principal reason is that a call option doesn't require the cash outlay that purchasing stock does. When you buy stock shares, you pay in full at the time of purchase. When you buy calls, you need only enough up-front cash to cover the writer's premium.

Buying puts

Same principles and advantages as buying calls, except here, the option buyer anticipates the value of the stock involved will decline.

Writing calls

Investors may write call options to generate income from the premiums earned in the transactions. Writing calls sometimes is used as a hedging strategy for stock already in the writer's portfolio. Should the value of the stock decline, the option will expire unexercised. The writer will pocket the premiums instead of getting nothing from the declining value of the stock. If the stock increases in value, the writer may have to sell some or all of it to meet the call but still will have the premiums as profit.

Writing puts

The writer generates income from premiums, and if the writer is covered, the downside is known and limited.

Buying straddles

A straddle is a combination of a put and a call on the same stock, with the same exercise date and strike price. In this scenario, the purchaser believes that the stock will be extremely volatile but can't forecast in which direction it will move or when. Each option, put and call, can be exercised separately, so movement in the share price must be large enough to cover the double premiums...and then some.

Selling straddles

As you might expect, this is the sale of a put and a call option on the same stock, with the same exercise date and strike price. The writer of the straddle believes that the stock will be quite stable, and as a result, the put or call consequences will be insignificant. Selling both options creates double the premium income.

Had enough jargon? If not, here are some other options-related terms you may encounter:

Strip

Two puts and a call on the same security.

Strap

You guessed it. Two calls and a put on the same stock.

Spreads

Spreads can occur when an investor buys *and* writes (sells) options on the same stock, with the transactions having one differing element. With a *money spread*, the strike price is different; with a *time spread*, the expiration date is different.

Scoring:

Score 4 points for b), 0 for any other answer. Buttons and bows aren't options-related terms yet, but stay tuned.

Question 2—

For which of these commodities can you purchase or sell *futures contracts*?

a) Coffee.

b) Wheat.

c) Pork bellies.

d) All of the above.

SPECIAL BONUS QUESTION:
In the film *Trading Places*, who portrayed the manservant of Dan Aykroyd and then Eddie Murphy after the two traded places?

a) Laird Cregar.

b) Ian Bannen.

c) Denholm Elliott.

d) Sting.

Why on earth, you're probably wondering, have we hit you with a piece of film trivia in this book about investing. There's method to our madness, and we'll reveal it in a moment as we discuss *futures contracts*.

In futures contracts, a buyer and a seller agree on a contract for the future exchange of an asset at a specified price, analogous to the strike price in options trading. Futures contracts typically involve commodities—corn, wheat, coffee, silver, soy beans, pork bellies, just to name a few. Most futures contracts are not exercised; they're traded instead, so a buyer seldom ends up with thousands of pork bellies slithering across the living room floor.

Futures contracts are basically bets on the future value of the commodities involved; in this regard, they work much the same as puts and calls. If wheat is trading at $50 and you're confident the price will rise to $100, you might purchase all the contracts you can at $50 or even higher because you'll profit when you sell the contracts for $100. Conversely, if you think the price of wheat will drop to $25, you lock in all the contracts you can to sell wheat at $50, because you'll buy it later at $25 and make your money on the difference.

Many of the hedging options that we noted with options are available in futures contracts. In addition, you can purchase futures contracts on stock market indexes, currencies, treasury bonds, and other assets—all without ever expecting to own those assets at the end of the day. To add yet another element of complexity, you can buy and sell options on futures contracts.

Now, to *Trading Places.* This film introduces viewers to the "pit," the nerve center of the Chicago Commodities Market, where the evil Duke brothers (Don Ameche and Ralph Bellamy), have found a way to steal confidential reports that would give them exclusive forecasts on crop harvests. Armed with this information, they alone would know whether commodities prices will rise or fall, and they stand to make a fortune in the appropriate futures contracts.

Enter the good guys (Aykroyd and Murphy), who thwart the Dukes' nefarious scheme by stealing the stolen reports before they reach the brothers, cornering the market themselves, and driving the Dukes to bankruptcy.

The movie's glimpse into the commodities market is Hollywoodesque, but its depiction of the pit—a chaotic, nerve-jangling nightmare where fortunes can be won or lost in a matter of hours or even moments—is real enough. The implied message of the film is that if you don't have secret information, futures trading demands sophistication and experience. If you try it without these traits, you may be trading places—with a pauper.

Scoring:

For Question 2, score 4 points for d), the best answer, 2 points for any other response.

For the Special Bonus Question, give yourself 1 point if you answered c) Denholm Elliott. By the way, Sting is not such a ridiculous answer as you might think. He and Elliott costarred in a 1982 movie called Brimstone and Treacle, a moody film about sex, guilt, and redemption—two of which are on display every day in the pit.

Question 3—

In investing, being "on margin" means:

a) You live on the fringes of society.

b) Your account is marginally profitable.

c) Your account is marginally unprofitable.

d) You're borrowing against the assets in your account to make additional asset purchases.

When you open an account at a brokerage, you typically can do so either with cash or by going on margin. Cash accounts are just what they seem—you buy stocks or bonds with cash, and your account is paid in full. In a margin account, you pay in cash only a portion of any purchase price, borrowing the balance from your broker, who uses the assets in your account as, in effect, collateral.

If you open such an account, you'll first encounter what's called the *initial margin*, the percentage in cash that you must provide to make a purchase. This rate is set by the Fed, which often uses it as a tool to regulate the economy. However, brokerage firms can require more then the minimum established by the Fed. If your broker requires an initial margin of 50 percent, for example, and you want to purchase $5,000 of a stock, you must provide $2,500 in cash. Your broker lends you the other $2,500.

Once you get past the initial margin, you'll find that most brokers require a *maintenance margin*, the percentage of equity that must be maintained in your account. If the maintenance margin is 30 percent, to cite one possibility, you must maintain at least 30 percent equity in a stock position or in your account as a whole. If your equity falls below 30 percent, the broker has the right to issue a *margin call*, requiring you to come up with enough cash to restore your account to the 30 percent equity level. If you can't, the broker may require you to sell enough of your stocks to restore the maintenance margin.

Margin trading can work for all parties involved. As the borrower, you get to leverage your assets and make purchases for which you might not otherwise have adequate or readily accessible cash. In theory, at least, your profits from these new assets more than compensate for the interest you're paying to your broker.

Brokerage firms benefit as well. Not only do they establish a revenue source from interest payments, but they also keep their customers active in the markets, which generates commissions.

But there are perils here. The obvious danger is that your interest rate may not be the most favorable rate available. Make sure you understand what your broker will charge you to use its money. If better rates are available elsewhere, there's little sense in borrowing from your broker.

The bigger risk is that you're playing in the market with paper money rather than cash, which can wreak havoc with your usual caution. If you must pay cash for a stock purchase, you consider it long and hard. If all you have to do to make that purchase is call your broker and advise him that you want to go on margin, you may not be as prudent in your decisions.

Margin calls *do* happen, and brokers *will* force you to sell your stock if necessary. There was a flurry of margin calls in the rapidly deteriorating markets of 2001–2002, forcing many involuntary stock sales. Margin calls create something of a self-fulfilling prophecy. A down market leads to margin call-related stock sales, which flood the market with securities, erode consumer confidence, and send the market into a deeper dive.

Scoring:

Score 4 points for d), 0 for any other answer.

Question 4—

Which of these statements about collectibles is true?

a) Collectibles make great investments because no matter their ultimate value, you acquire things you enjoy.

b) Collectibles make great assets because they always appreciate in value.

c) Collectibles make great assets because they're easy to sell.

d) All of the above.

Collectibles—antiques, coins, stamps, first-edition books, paintings, baseball cards, Barbie dolls are just a few categories—represent another type of exotic investment. Many people get into collectibles primarily for pleasure. They like the hunt, they cherish the items they acquire, and they *really* like preserving, categorizing, and recategorizing their treasures. Some even dedicate their lives to collecting, and to them we say: God speed. Personal fulfillment always should be the driving force in collectibles.

But collectibles tend to be problematic when viewed primarily as investments. The first snag is that they don't always grow in value. You may purchase the work of an artist who's the darling of the docent set today, but who knows how the artist's work will be perceived years from now? And who knows how many works by that artist ultimately will reach the market? If the market is flooded with paintings by the artist whose work you've purchased, the value of your holdings could drop substantially.

Or consider the rocky ride of baseball cards. Their value sizzled in the 1980s and early 1990s, only to fizzle thereafter. Many shows and small-time collectors folded their tents when the card market tanked. Where value is concerned, collectibles work pretty much as other assets. They have their booms and busts, and no one knows for sure which is coming next.

Yet another challenge is the potential illiquidity of your collectibles. When owners of major art collections want to cash out, they can turn to prominent auction houses for dispersal sales. But if you're ready to sell your collection of classic jukeboxes or lawn jockeys, who will arrange an auction for you?

More often than not, you're left to devise and implement a dispersal scheme yourself. That means time, money, and probably less at the bottom line.

If you're determined to pursue collectibles as investments, consider these measures as part of the process:

Thoroughly research the field

Articulate and understand both your goals and the risks involved. Ask yourself these questions: What costs are involved in collecting? How long do I plan to keep these assets? What exit strategy will I employ? What appreciation and depreciation potential exists? Ask tough questions, as you would with any other investment.

Use your research to learn how to value the collectibles you encounter. What criteria determine the value? If you know that, you're less likely to overspend, less likely to be victimized by fraud.

Purchase appropriate insurance

Don't assume that your homeowners insurance covers your collectibles. Most policies require riders for such items—jewelry included. Remember to add the premiums to the projected costs of your enterprise.

Have your collection appraised

When the value of your collection is appraised, that enhances its credibility and can make selling it an easier task. Appraisals also are useful for estate planning; when you know what your collection is worth, you're better able to decide how—and to whom—to bequeath it. Also, your heirs will know the value of what you're leaving them, so they won't give their inheritance away or leave it under mounds of dusty boxes and old clothing in the attic.

Use an independent appraiser—one with no ties to you or the collectibles themselves—to avoid the appearance of conflict of interest. And when you're considering the purchase of a collectible, ask to see an appraisal. It works on the buying and selling end.

Don't forget taxes

If you sell any of your collectibles, remember that the proceeds usually are taxable. This is true whether you sell the items yourself or employ a professional broker or auctioneer. It's important to note that the reduction in capital gains tax rates that we experienced in 2001 does not apply to collectibles. Capital gains on collectibles are taxed at 28 percent or 15 percent (if you're in the 15 percent bracket).

Keep detailed records of your sales as well as your acquisition and installation costs. These expenses will help offset profits and reduce your tax bill.

It's wonderful to imagine that one of your thousands of baseball cards turns out to be the only surviving picture of Ted Williams batting right-handed, worth millions and assuring you a cushy future. But just in case it doesn't work out that way, collect things that, first and foremost, bring you pleasure. If it turns out that they bring you profit as well, so much the better.

Scoring:

Score 4 points for a), 0 for any other answer.

Scoring for Chapter 13		
	Highest Possible Score	**Your Score**
Question 1	4	_____
Question 2	4	_____
Bonus Question	1	_____
Question 3	4	_____
Question 4	4	_____
CHAPTER TOTALS	17	_____

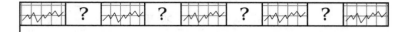

14

Your Investing IQ— You Know What You Know...and What You Need to Know

I f you've stuck with us for 13 chapters, you have a pretty good sense of where your investing knowledge is strong and where you may need some work. Most novice investors, and even some veterans, find that they excel in certain areas, while lagging behind in others. The danger is that you'll focus exclusively on strategies and assets that you know, missing plenty of opportunities in the asset classes and subclasses that remain unfamiliar to you. Your mission is to become familiar with all of them.

To determine your Investing IQ, enter your marks for each chapter in the grid on page 240, add all 13 chapter scores to determine your total, then check out your ranking in the categories on page 241.

Investing IQ Score

	Highest Possible Score	Your Score
Chapter 1	16	_____
Chapter 2	16	_____
Chapter 3	18	_____
Chapter 4	18	_____
Chapter 5	18	_____
Chapter 6	16	_____
Chapter 7	16	_____
Chapter 8	20	_____
Chapter 9	16	_____
Chapter 10	16	_____
Chapter 11	20	_____
Chapter 12	16	_____
Chapter 13	17	_____
GRAND TOTAL	223	_____

Investing Categories

▣ Investing Ace
Score of 201–223

You got at least 90 percent of the total possible score—you're likely a successful investor already or poised to become one. Hey, Ace, call us when you get ready for a major buy so we can tag along for the ride.

▣ Grand Pooh-bah in Training
Score of 168–200

You scored at least 75 percent, meaning you have a solid but still imperfect grounding in investing. With some regular research and the commitment of a little more effort, you'll be ready for prime time.

▣ Student of the Game
Score of 112–167

You were right at least 50 percent of the time. In baseball, that gets you first-ballot induction into the Hall of Fame; in investing, 50 percent may not be a good enough batting average. Now that you know what you know—and what you still need to know—dedicate your time to filling in the gaps.

▣ Potential Victim
Score of 111 or less

Alas, you're lost in the econo-mist, adrift on the Sure-Cash-Owe Sea. The best strategy for you is to give us all your discretionary money and let us invest it for you. We'll let you know how you do.

We're kidding, of course, but that's just the sort of pitch to which you're susceptible if you don't have adequate knowledge about investing. If you scored less than 50 percent, you need some serious study before committing your hard-earned resources to an investing plan.

Do it now. If you find that your understanding of investing isn't what you thought or hoped it was, don't despair, and don't give up. That would be tantamount to abandoning your goals, which is a defeatist attitude you never want to adopt. Treat your low score as a wake-up call and determine to learn more. Investing is the best way to achieve your goals; doing so from a solid foundation of information and understanding is the best way to invest.

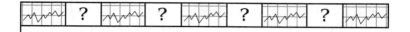

Bibliography

Books

Morningstar Mutual Funds User's Guide.

Bernstein, Leopold A. *Financial Statement Analysis: Theory, Application, and Interpretation*, 4th edition. New York: Richard D. Irwin, 1989.

Bernstein, William. *The Intelligent Asset Allocator*. New York: McGraw-Hill, 2001.

Galbraith, John Kenneth. *A Short History of Financial Euphoria*. New York: Viking Penguin, 1993.

Gardner, David and Tom Gardner. *The Motley Fool Investment Workbook*. New York: Fireside, 1998.

Gibson, Roger C. *Asset Allocation—Balancing Financial Risk*. New York: McGraw-Hill, 2000.

Lynch, Peter and John Rothchild (contributor). *One Up On Wall Street—How to Use What You Already Know to Make Money in the Market*. New York: Simon & Schuster, 1989.

Martin, Carrie Coghill and Evan M. Pattak. *The Newlyweds' Guide to Investing & Personal Finance.* Franklin Lakes, N.J.: Career Press, 2002.

Mobius, Mark, *The Investor's Guide to Emerging Markets.* New York: Irwin Professional Publishing, 1995.

Mundy, Floyd W. *The Value of a Railroad Security* New York: American Institute of Finance, 1920.

Siegel, Jeremy J., *Stocks for the Long Run.* New York: McGraw-Hill, 1998.

Web Sites

About.com *(stocks.about.com)*

American Stock Exchange *(www.amex.com)*

AmosWEB e Tutor *(www.AmosWEB.com)*

Bank for International Settlements *(www.bis.org)*

Barra, Inc. *(www.barra.com)*

Biz/ed *(www.bized.ac.uk/)*

BondsOnline *(www.bondsonline.com)*

The Conference Board—Indicators *(www.globalindicators.org)*

Contingency Analysis *(www.contingencyanalysis.com)*

Encarta *(encarta.msn.com)*

FundAdvice.com *(www.fundadvice.com)*

International Forum on Globalization *(www.ifg.org)*

International Monetary Fund *(www.imf.org)*

The Internationalist—The Center for International Business & Travel *(www.internationalist.com)*

Kiplinger.com *(www.kiplinger.com)*

Libertyhaven.com *(www.libertyhaven.com)*

Money in My Mattress *(www.moneyinmymattress.com*)

MX Moneyextra *(www.mxmoneyextra.com)*

NASDAQ Stock Market *(www.nasdaq.com)*
New York Stock Exchange *(www.nyse.com)*
Putnam Investments *(www.putnaminvestments.com)*
TaxPlanet *(www.taxplanet.com)*
U.S. Securities and Exchange Commission *(www.sec.gov)*
World Trade Organization *(www.wto.org)*

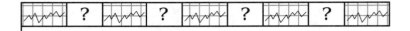

Index

About the Authors

CARRIE L. COGHILL is president, certified financial planner, and co-founder of D.B. Root & Company, a financial planning firm based in Pittsburgh. She has more than 16 years of experience in the financial services industry and specializes in counseling "new American millionaires"—those with a sudden realization that they have substantial funds to invest and little or no experience in doing so.

"It's our job to help them establish and implement the right investment strategies for their lives," Coghill says. "Ours is a very one-on-one business."

As a registered representative with Commonwealth Financial Network, Inc., and as a licensed insurance agent and a registered investment advisor, she counsels clients in the areas of investment management, retirement planning, and estate planning.

Coghill's distinguished career in financial planning has brought her considerable recognition. She is a frequent commentator on CNBC's *Power Lunch* and serves as co-host for

Financial Planning, a twice-monthly program on Pittsburgh NBC affiliate WPXI-TV. She was selected in December 1998 as one of the nation's "Ace Advisors" by *Ticker* magazine.

Her investment advice was quoted extensively in the June 1999 cover story of *Working Mother* magazine. She also has been quoted by such publications as *The Wall Street Journal Europe, Martha Stewart Living, Woman's Day, Brides, Investor's Business Journal, Small Business News, Dayton Daily News,* and *Stages,* a magazine of personal finance. She serves as contributing editor for *Physicians' News Digest.* On broadcast and cable television, she has been featured on *Bloomberg TV, The Ananda Lewis Show,* and *Simplify Your Life.*

She served as a retirement planning expert for the Website *www.Quote.com,* and she regularly presents workshops and participates in other forums to educate the public about investments and financial planning, always taking the "consumer advocate" approach.

She earned a degree in finance and accounting from Robert Morris College—now Robert Morris University—in Pittsburgh and is a past vice president of the college's Alumni Association Executive Council. She is president emeritus of the Pittsburgh Chapter of the International Association of Financial Planning (IAFP), and she serves on the board of directors for the Pennsylvania Partnership for Education.

E van **M. Pattak**, a Pittsburgh native, is a writer, editor, publicist, and teacher, among other pursuits. He is co-author of *Insiders' Guide to Pittsburgh,* and his magazine writing has won Golden Quill and Women in Communications Matrix Awards and was anthologized in *Our Roots Grow Deeper Than We Know,* a collection featuring Pennsylvania writers.

He served as editor-in-chief of *Executive Report,* a former monthly business magazine in Pittsburgh, and as acting editor of *The University of Pittsburgh Campaign Chronicle,* and he operates a public relations agency serving such clients as the Urban Redevelopment Authority of Pittsburgh.

His writing appears regularly in such publications as *T.E.Q.,* the magazine of the Pittsburgh Technology Council, and *PA Manufacturer.* He served for 16 years as public relations director of the cable television franchise in Pittsburgh, which was operated initially by Warner Amex Cable, then by its successor, TCI of Pennsylvania, Inc. He began his career as a reporter for the Associated Press.

For more than two decades, he served on the adjunct writing faculty at Seton Hill College in Greensburg, PA., teaching journalism, magazine writing, and oral history.

He is an official scorer for Major League Baseball and is proud to have scored a League Championship Series, an All-Star Game, and a no-hitter. He serves as part-time host and handicapper for the Meadows Racing Network and acknowledges that as a handicapper, he's a great editor.

He was graduated from the University of Pittsburgh with a B.A. in Political Science. He and his wife, Pohla Smith, reside in the Park Place neighborhood of Pittsburgh.